VLORs & VICE:
Rise of a BIO-Being

VLORs & VICE:
Rise of a BIO-Being
— VOLUME 2 —

Sean L Johnson

VLORS & VICE: RISE OF A BIO-BEING
VOLUME 2

*This is a work of fiction. All of the characters, names, incidents,
organizations, and dialogue in this novel are either the products
of the author's imagination or are used fictitiously.*

iUniverse books may be ordered through booksellers or by contacting:

iUniverse
1663 Liberty Drive
Bloomington, IN 47403
www.iuniverse.com
844-349-9409

*Because of the dynamic nature of the Internet, any web addresses or
links contained in this book may have changed since publication and
may no longer be valid. The views expressed in this work are solely those
of the author and do not necessarily reflect the views of the publisher,
and the publisher hereby disclaims any responsibility for them.*

ISBN: 978-1-4917-9850-8 (sc)
ISBN: 978-1-4917-9849-2 (e)

Library of Congress Control Number: 2015917038

Print information available on the last page.

iUniverse rev. date: 04/04/2023

Prologue

Deep in outer space, in an unknown galaxy, stars were exploding and ripping themselves apart. Something was causing this to happen.

The catastrophic event started before our heroes were born, and the early stages weren't that serious about being detected by astronomers and scientists on planet Earth.

In the beginning, stars were slowly aligning themselves in an odd pattern. Then, they would explode! The stars only burst one by one. Then, coming into the New Year, 2107, silent bursts went off. Multiple stars were exploding, going, poof, and was happening far away from planet Neptune. Astronomers learned about this in early January 2107.

Suddenly, on February 21st, 2107, there was a burst of light and an unusual crackling noise. A star shot away from an unknown galaxy and became a stream of light. This light traveled great distances in a short time. The stream of light flew past many asteroid fields, passing many moons and unseen planets. Finally, the light aimed toward planet Earth and struck at the heart of HighTech City, Georgia.

It happened so fast. Many people felt blinded by the strange cosmic light that filled many areas around the city. The mysterious light lasted only a few seconds and genetically altered many.

While the stars were ripping themselves apart, two things traveled simultaneously but in different dimensions.

A mysterious metal sheet was floating in deep space, somewhere in the Namorant Dimension. An alien named DiLuAH was traveling away from his home world, planet Vegues, to escape punishment for the crimes. The alien's planet is in the Isolated Dimension, trillions of miles away from Earth.

The two were traveling side by side but in two different dimensions. DiLuAH's powers created a magical doorway that made a rip in time and space—the alien's powers connected to the mysterious sheet of metal floating in the Namorant Dimension, and it came to the Isolated Dimension.

DiLuAH opened his eyes, gazed out of the window of his ship, and saw something appear before his eyes in the form of a blinding white light. Suddenly, asteroids struck the ship and the mysterious metal sheet; it crashed on planet Earth in 2080. A few years later, DiLuAH's ship recovered from its malfunction in outer space, and his ship's controls steered to planet Earth.

In 2085, his ship made a crash landing near Sysis June Lake in Naphilia Town, Illinois. The alien crawled out of his spaceship and made it to a safe distance. He turned slightly to his right, looking at his damaged ship, and watched it explode.

The light that struck HighTech City, and affected five individuals, was just the beginning; it also struck near Hidendale Springs, Illinois. Mageario's deep slumber had been disturbed. His tomb cracked open, and he awakened thanks to a slight earthquake. Thirteen years later, this cursed knight crawled out from under Drenden Mountain.

The rip in time and space created a meltdown. This meltdown eventually caused several planets, on both ends, to be affected in strange ways.

On Wednesday, March 01st, 2107, terrible and unusual weather started on planet Vrec. Imprisoned enemies attacked prince Zanari, and he fled to Earth in search of a friend.

Season 2, Episode 9:
Continued from Book 1

At the end of book one, Zadarion is at Hidendale Observatory in Hidendale Springs, Illinois. Unbeknownst to him, there is a secret agent within the group of students. Techy Andy is incognito, hiding in plain sight as a tourist participating in the civilian tour.

Friday, June 9, 2107

There are two tours, the first-year class from Centransdale High School and the civilian tour. Techy Andy plans on retrieving the newest invention, The BIO-Being. But first, he must find out its location.

The tour guide, Cynthia Hadolsby, shows the students around the Planetary Unit. The exhibit depicts eight original planets, with twelve more discovered in 2050.

Techy Andy, disguised as a scientist, is searching for and assisting fellow scientists. He is a nerd, so he has become distracted by his main task.

Meanwhile, Mr. Curtis Anaheim is walking down a hallway on the second floor. Moments later, a young man runs up to him and calls his name from down the hall.

MORALES EWELLING. *Running down the hall, approaching Mr. Anaheim while calling out his name.* Mr. Anaheim! Mr. Anaheim! *He makes it to him and stops running, catching his breath.*

MR. ANAHEIM. *Stops walking and turns around. He looks at the young teenager.* Ah. Mr. Ewelling's son. How has my good friend Tom been doing? *Smiles.*

MORALES EWELLING. *He blows air out of his mouth and rolls his eyes.* He's doing well. Anyway...

MR. ANAHEIM. Yes?

MORALES EWELLING. I want the opportunity to be your understudy. Sir! Before you answer... I have been your biggest fan. I just graduated from Centransdale High. Your company is where I belong. Please. Allow me to work under you and shadow you.

MR. ANAHEIM. You realize dozens of people idolize my inventions. Some individuals, the majority are applicants, even try to infiltrate my company and try to buy me with the same spill you're giving me right now. *He looks at him suspiciously.*

MORALES EWELLING. Sir. I am no thief and wish to know how you run your company. I design products, too, even though they're still in the planning phase. But, please. Consider hiring me as an intern. I'll take the trash out and clean your car. I'll do anything!

MR. ANAHEIM. *He thinks for a minute and taps a button on his watch.*

Three security guards come to the second floor and escort him out of the building.

MORALES EWELLING. Sir! Please! *Being dragged away from Anaheim.*

MR. ANAHEIM. Place a request at Anaheim Industries next time. *He turns around and starts walking downstairs to a secured room.*

He walks down the stairs and sees a closed door with a security identification box on the door. He verifies who he is, the door slides open, and a security guard, who's standing watch, welcomes him inside.

UNNAMED SECURITY GUARD. *He nods his head.* All conditions are normal, sir.

MR. CURTIS ANAHEIM. *Returns the head nod.* Thank you, Watch stander. *Looks around the room.* Where is it?

UNNAMED SECURITY GUARD. To your right, sir. My superiors wanted it concealed as much as possible.

MR. CURTIS ANAHEIM. *He's looking at the giant-sized crate.* Nice. *He turns his body, facing the guard.* I have two maintenance guys arriving from Anaheim Industries to pick it up.

UNNAMED SECURITY GUARD. Sir, with all due respect, should we utilize the back exit?

MR. CURTIS ANAHEIM. *He laughs. Then he pats the security guard once on the shoulder.* My friend, why make it so obvious? *He smiles while he exits the room.* Take care of this; I'm counting on you. *The door slides shut behind him.*

Anaheim makes his way down the hall, passing many room spaces. He uses the other stairwell. He makes his way up the long flight of stairs, stops at the top, and watches the students walking with Mrs. Hadolsby pass in front of him, going into another exhibit.

The woman has a lot of enthusiasm in her voice than when the students first arrived. As they pass him, Zadarion turns his head to get another look at him. The boy turns his head back quickly, looking ahead. Another person in the group looked at the man as well, suspiciously.

Anaheim starts walking down the other end of the hallway. He comes close to an open room, and a scientist is backing out. The scientist almost bumps into him.

MR. CURTIS ANAHEIM. Ahem.

UNNAMED SCIENTIST. *He stops and turns his head.* My apologies, sir.

MR. CURTIS ANAHEIM. *He looks at his nametag and tries to pronounce it correctly.* Mr. Areeoles Miles?

UNNAMED SCIENTIST. *He corrects him: Ariolas* Miles, sir.

MR. CURTIS ANAHEIM. I am sorry. I butcher names. *He fixes his shirt collar.* Carry on, Mr. Miles. Keep up the excellent work. *He continues walking down the hall, heading toward the exit.*

He exits the hallway, and Mr. Ariolas Miles peeks out of the room.

MR. ARIOLAS MILES. *He grins.* Lovely meeting you for the first time, my hero. *He gets back to work.* Let's begin! *He smirks and raises his right arm, revealing a tablet computer on his right wrist.*

Meanwhile, DiLusion approaches Morgan Wiles in the dark dimension. The teen girl is working hard at her small station—the only thing in the room beside a few newly built steel walls, and the space is a vast opened space of nothing.

DILUSION. Any progress?

MORGAN WILES. *She points to her left, then lowers her arm and continues working.* Over there.

DILUSION. *Smiles.* You will be going out in the field with my young apprentice soon. *The smile fades from his face.*

MORGAN WILES. *She acts surprised.* I'm a science nerd, not a warrior!

DILUSION. *Starts grinning.* Please explain to me again what you did to Shocker before you injected him with that drug you created.

MORGAN WILES. Okay. But if I'm going out there, I would like to be called, Flurir. *She pauses.* It's partially the name of my creation. *Smiling.*

DiLusion chuckles, and then he disappears into a portal. She looks away and gets back to work.

FLURIR. *Stops smiling.* I'm starting to like it here!

ShaVenger is concealing himself in the darkness, controlling his breathing. He hears and shakes his head.

In Kale County, Illinois, after watching a high school football team at practice, Rani Darivele starts walking home. At the same time, He is throwing his football high in the air and catching it.

After twenty minutes, he makes it home. He opens the door, steps inside, and places the football on the floor underneath the coat hooks.

RANI. Hm? Mom and dad must still be at work. I wonder if Dani is with them.

He walks to his bedroom (also his twin sister's room). He opens the bedroom door. He sees her working on their computer, holding the mysterious gaming console the two of them found.

RANI. *He sneaks up behind her for a scare. He shouts.* Yo sis, what are you doing!?

DANI. *She jerks her body around in her chair and drops the gaming console.* Oh my God! What is wrong with you? *Sighs and picks up the device, checking for any scratches.*

RANI. *He sits down in the chair next to her.* I got your butt! Ha-ha!! *Laughing hard.*

DANI. You are lucky this gaming console doesn't have a scratch on it. I would *so* be on the floor whooping yo' butt right now!

RANI. *He laughs.* Yeeeah right! You would have to catch me, slowpoke! *He stops playing around and gets serious.* What are you working on?

DANI. *She sighs and shakes her head, facing him, holding the gaming console.* Do you remember that weird guy who bumped into you and dropped this?

RANI. Uh-huh.

DANI. Rani, this isn't a gaming console from 1991. *Smiling.*

RANI. *He becomes nervous about the way she's looking at him.* Why are you staring at me like that?

DANI. *She punches his right arm and raises her voice.* That's why stupid!!

RANI. Ow! *He rubs his arm.*

DANI. That's what you get. Please don't play with me! *She starts laughing and winks at him.*

RANI. Sneaky. And I am *not* stupid; you're stupid!

DANI. Shuuuut up! *Smiles. She spins her chair around, so she is facing their computer.* Just listen, Bro-bro. This is what we needed to complete Virt World.

RANI. *He raises his voice.* Oh shit! Really?

DANI. *She shakes her head.* Mom didn't teach you yet about your mouth?

RANI. I still have the scars, so ... *He sticks his tongue out and laughs.* I'm kidding.

DANI. No, you're not.

RANI. You right. *He shakes his head three times fast.* So yeah!? *He's excited.* Virt World is a Go-Go?

DANI. *She is excited too.* Yes!!

RANI. Let me help you out; you're an amateur. *He starts working on the dual computer. He opens a file and modifies the blueprints to their "Virt World" design.* Thank... you... mystery guy!

Back in Hidendale Springs, Illinois, inside Hidendale Observatory, the time is now four o'clock in the evening, and the tour is about to end. Techy Andy, disguised as Ariolas Miles, makes his way to the lower level, carrying quite a few boxes to trick the cameras.

He walks to the secured room, places the boxes on the floor, and pulls out a digital card with Anaheim's eyes showing on the front.

He intentionally bumped into him. As Anaheim looked him in the eyes, a photo was taken and stored in the scientist's glasses.

He enters the security codes and personal data; then, the door slides open. He immobilizes the guard on duty, beginning his search. After looking through six of seven wooden crates, he finds what he was sent to the Observatory to retrieve. He opens the seventh crate and discovers a nail-sized USB device. He picks it up and plugs it into his encrypted tablet, located on his right wrist. He has all kinds of measures to prevent malware from uploading to his tablet.

He locates the folder and double-taps using his left pointer finger. The folder opens in a new window, showing blueprints, and there is a digital body embedded in the blueprints.

Two maintenance workers enter the Observatory on the main floor and head downstairs; they are here to pick up and take the package to Anaheim Industries.

They arrive at the secured room with Anaheim. He opens the door. The intruder stops what he's doing and continues looking at his tablet.

TECHY ANDY. *Smiling. The first* time I got caught! *He starts laughing.*

One of the maintenance guys decides to take him down. Andy swipes his left palm across his tablet screen and unleashes a digital microchip. It enters a broken vacuum cleaner, and the tech makes it come alive and goes on a rampage. The intruder runs out of the room, pushing Anaheim onto the floor. The nail-sized USB device falls out of his tablet on the floor. Anaheim covers the device with his right hand. Andy raises his right arm, signaling the vacuum bot to attack.

Suddenly, a Dabney Dart flies past his right ear. Andy lowers his right arm and turns around to face the newcomer.

TECHY ANDY. *Displeased. He sneers.* Damn. *He whispered.* I didn't want you guys— *He raises his voice.* —interfering!

AGENT CQUA. *Starts walking toward the man, speaking French.* Ah. Pourquoi si déprimé? (Ah. Why so depressed?) *Starts smiling.*

Anaheim gets to his feet with the USB in his right hand and then runs to the exit. The vacuum bot exits the secure room and goes after him. The newcomer stops walking and continues to look at Techy Andy.

The man runs so fast downstairs, and he falls on his face when he reaches the ground floor. The students turn their heads to see. Mrs. Hadolsby runs to the man.

The vacuum bot arrives on the ground floor, landing in front of the man and the woman. The woman freaks out! The man is eyeing the robot while simultaneously trying to pull himself off the floor using Hadolsby as support.

The vacuum bot roars. The students are terrified, and they are panicking.

Zadarion sneaks away, running into a nearby utility closet. He double-checks if the area is clear before transforming.

The vacuum bot starts to approach Mrs. Hadolsby and Mr. Anaheim. Agent Z teleports outside the Observatory and then flies inside through the ceiling. He throws out his left foot, kicking the robot. The vacuum bot falls on its back, and Z lands in front of the adults.

AGENT Z. Get behind me. *He shouts.* Now!!!!

The vacuum bot stands up and speeds toward Z.

The agent materializes his sword and starts running. He slashes the robot's extension cord and slices off its robotic arms and legs. He jumps on top of the robot and stabs it in its chest. The vacuum bot loses its balance, and Z jumps off, landing on one knee.

AGENT Z. *He thinks to himself.* I cannot do an Invisi-Dome right now.

He throws a V-Inducer. The device enlarges and closes itself around the vacuum bot. He de-materializes his sword and materializes his blaster, shooting the center of the device. It activates. The vacuum bot explodes inside the V-Inducer. The device returns to his V-Link. The agent glides outside and then throws out an Invisi-Dome.

The mystery agent blocks Techy Andy's attempted kick on the second floor. The mystery agent looks out the window.

AGENT CQUA. An Invisi-Dome? *He picks the man up and throws him next to the flight of stairs.*

TECHY ANDY. Shit! *He activates his flight device and flies out the window.*

AGENT CQUA. *Speaking French.* Vous allez nulle part. (You are going nowhere.) *Smiles.*

The agent walks to the window and materializes a giant sword. He manually changes it into a blaster, points it out the window, and shoots at the man's flight backpack. Techy Andy swerved to his left at the last second, flying low and landing on the ground. The agent jumps out the window and lands on the ground. He positions his blaster, pointing it at the enemy, and reshoots him.

The young man uses his laptop to activate his shield and quickly raises his arm to block the attack. The force of the blast knocks him on his butt.

The agent de-materializes the blaster and speed runs. The boy grabs Andy and throws him over his shoulder, and he flies into the Observatory's first-floor window. The man breaks through the glass and falls on the floor, landing a few feet away from students, including the tour guide and Anaheim.

After searching upstairs, Z runs downstairs to check out the noise. He stares at Techy Andy as the man gets to his feet.

AGENT Z. *He is looking at him. Confused.* Who are you?

AGENT CQUA. *He jumps through the broken window before it repairs itself, thanks to the restoration abilities of the activated Invisi-Dome. He is holding his blaster in his right hand. Speaks French.* Appelez-le Techy Andy. (Call him Techy Andy.) *Starts talking in English.* Hello, friend. *Smiling.*

AGENT Z. *His eyes become wide.* And who are you?

AGENT CQUA. Agent CQua. *Smiling.*

TECHY ANDY. *He dives at Anaheim.* Give the USB drive to me now! *He demanded.*

AGENT CQUA. I'll talk to you later! *He points his blaster and fires it.*

AGENT Z. *He moves out of the way.* Whooooaaaa!!!

The intruder intentionally falls to the ground to avoid the blast. The attack steers off course because it lost its intended target, striking the ceiling. Andy snatches the USB device out of the man's hand and plugs it into his tablet. Z jumps in closer and starts throwing punches. Techy Andy gets hit by a few and avoids the rest. Z attempts to snatch the USB out of the laptop, but he's punched across the right side of his face. CQua jumps in to battle. The young man uses the other agent as a shield and pushes Z into CQua.

TECHY ANDY. That's enough!! *He points his laptop, a laser gun, at the agents.* You followed me to America. Now, you die, secret agent!

He fires it, and Z steps in front of the blast and, at the same time, materializes his shield. The shot hits with tremendous impact.

The young agent felt a million volts of some energy pass through him, almost like electrocution.

CQua raises his giant blaster and shoots the man in his chest, and he falls to the floor. *The foreign agent turns to look at his comrade.*

Z has his left hand on the upper part of his right arm, holding the mysterious metallic armband.

AGENT CQUA. You good, pal? *He is looking at him.*

AGENT Z. Yeah. *He stutters.* It— It felt like my soul was leaving my body.

Anaheim notices something forming into a human in front of him. This new form looks just like the agent but with minor differences. It has blue and grayish hair. He's sporting the same uniform, but it's in a lighter shade. The new form has a visor that covers his eyes.

??????. Soul? *Laughing.* I didn't know we had one. *Stops laughing and winks his left eye.*

MR. CURTIS ANAHEIM. No way. A materialized artificial intelligence. *He is astonished.*

The two agents stare at Anaheim; they then stare at the new being in the room. Techy Andy stands up, and CQua materializes V-Cuffs and tosses them at him. They wrap around his body, but they do not immobilize him.

AGENT CQUA. *He snatches the USB out of the man's tablet. He turns his attention to the new person in the center of the room. Speaks French.* Le fantôme de grand César. (Great Caesar's ghost.) *Speaks in English.* Why does he look like you?! *He looks at Z, then at the clone.*

??????. I deny such accusation— *He points at Z.* —that I look like that disgusting creature!

AGENT Z. *Shouts angrily.* Shut it!!

??????. *Laughs.* Call me Curdur, brother! *Bows while grinning.*

AGENT CQUA. How did the USB do that?

MR. CURTIS ANAHEIM. It's not the USB drive, but what's inside it.

AGENT Z. Please explain, sir.

MR. CURTIS ANAHEIM. Yes. Inside the USB are tiny bits of code. The "BIO-Beings" is a new technology to reduce how many Americans enlist in the military. With these digital beings, a person can clone him or herself multiple times.

CURDUR. My God. You're a terrible storyteller. *Chuckles.*

MR. CURTIS ANAHEIM. *Turns to look at BIO-Being.* Also, a person must sacrifice a part of themselves.

CURDUR. Ok. You can die now! *He raises his right arm, equipped with an arm blaster.*

AGENT Z. No!! *He jumps in front, materializes his sword, and deflects the blast.*

The digital clone runs to the teen agent. He throws punches, and Z swings his weapon to avoid the blows. Curdur grabs Z's sword kicks him in his abdomen, and leaps back, landing seven steps away.

Curdur's holding the sword with two hands now. After analyzing it, he snaps it in half like nothing.

AGENT CQUA. Whoa!

AGENT Z. *Shouts.* Hey?!

Curdur charges forward and throws several punches. Z leaps backward to avoid them and hits a wall— Z groans. The other agent is studying this new enemy.

The clone speeds at Z, raises his right fist and is about to strike.

The boy stands up straight, raises his right arm, and he knocks his arm away from him. They start going at it aggressively.

The enemy grabs Z's waist and slams him onto the floor; he moans but quickly gets to his feet.

Z stares as Curdur stare back, smiling.

CURDUR. Let me show you a trick. *He grins.*

He speeds forward and grabs Z's throat. He can feel Curdur's hand squeezing tight around his neck. The clone has one tight grip, using only his right hand. He takes him for a ride, speeding forward and pushing Z backward. The two of them go through the buildings wall and the Invisi-Dome barrier faster than the speed of sound.

The other agent quickly passes the USB to Anaheim and follows. Anaheim stares at the same wall after CQua leaves for some time.

The Invisi-Dome went away.

The man takes the woman and children to the lounge five seconds later. He noticed that all the school students, including Mrs. Hadolsby, had dreamy-like eyes.

Meanwhile, on Drenden Mountain, behind the observatory, Curdur forces Z into the dirt and lets go of his neck. He walks over to the edge and stares down the mountain. They are five hundred feet from the ground. Z slowly gets to his feet, looking at him. The enemy has his back turned. The agent tries to materialize his sword, but nothing happens.

CURDUR. *He speaks with excitement.* Ready for another round?! *He laughs and turns his body to face the agent.*

AGENT Z. What are you talking about— it's still round one!

The foreign agent makes his way to Drenden Mountain. While in the air, he soon spots the duplicates. He uses his V-Link and teleport, reappearing an inch away from the enemy clone, reaching for his neck in succession. Curdur has the same goofy smile on his face.

AGENT Z. *Seeing the smile on his clone's face.* CQua!!

AGENT CQUA. Don't worry. I got him!

The clone grabs his left arm and flips him over his shoulder. The agent is lying on his back. The enemy goes in for another blow, throwing his left fist down. Z speeds in and throws his right leg out.

Curdur is quick! He stops his attack, grabs his right leg with his right hand, and throws him twenty feet away. Z falls on his back. CQua gets to his feet and starts throwing punches. Curdur dodges every last one, grinning. He grabs CQua's fists and jumps in the air, taking the agent with him. Curdur knees him in his chin and releases him. CQua falls and smacks into the dirt.

The foreign agent gets to his hands and knees. The enemy stares at him and then turns his head to look at Z.

The two agents stand. CQua backs away from Curdur, watching him cautiously.

CURDUR. *He raises his arms in a confused expression.* What? *He is grinning evilly.* Is that it?

AGENT CQUA. *He materializes his large blaster sword and points it at the enemy. He shouts.* Not by a long shot!!! *He fires.*

The blast hits. Curdur turned his head to look at CQua, and then the attack hit him.

AGENT CQUA. *He lowers his weapon and speaks in French.* Rendez-vous jamais perdant (See you never, loser).

The smoke is starting to clear. Z spots a silhouette pointing something in CQua's direction inside the disappearing smoke.

AGENT Z. *He shouts.* Look out!! *He activates the hovering ability in his boots and flies closer to stop him.*

The doppelganger fires an attack from the arm blaster on his right arm at CQua. The agent stands his ground, comfortably positioning his body. He raises his right arm, and his shield materializes in front of him. The attack hits.

Agent Z reaches the enemy and punches him across his face. Curdur's right arm falls. Z kicks him in his abdomen, uses two hands, and uppercuts him high. CQua jumps high, fires an attack, and Curdur takes the hit. Within a second, the enemy flies out of the smoke and punches CQua in his stomach. The impact was very effective. The agent's insides felt like they were going to escape out of his body. He falls out of the sky.

Z uses the hovering ability in his boots and flies at his clone, and Curdur turns around and aims at him. The two clashes, both knocked out of the sky and hit the ground, creating crater-sized holes.

CQua is on his hands and knees and still feeling pain in his midsection. He starts slowly crawling on the ground to where the other two landed.

Z pulls himself off the ground. Curdur stands up and launches at him. Z puts up a defensive posture, blocking his punch. The two of them start going blow for blow. They are equal, but Z is becoming exhausted. Curdur is looking well-rested. CQua stands up, slowly limping to where the fighting is taking place.

CURDUR. *He blocks an incoming punch and forces Z's right arm behind his back. He has him in a tight spot and starts smiling.* Look at you. All mighty and full of persistence! *He laughs.* Tell you what. I will easily remove my hand from your soon-to-be torn-off appendage if you decide to give it up. Deal brother?

AGENT Z. *He struggles.* We are *not* brothers!

CURDUR. I wanted a different response.

AGENT Z. Give what up? Ahhh! *He struggles not to move because his arm is hurting terribly.*

CURDUR. *He twists his wrist a little, enough so that he is in more pain.* Answer my question again, brother. *Grinning menacingly.*

The agent remains quiet. He is trying to stay relaxed, so he won't feel the pain Curdur is inflicting on him.

The other foreign agent continues limping to where the fight is taking place. He soon falls on his face but gets on his hands and knees, determined not to give up.

Agent Z is still refusing to answer the question. Suddenly, a dagger flies past Curdur's left leg and cuts him deep. He held in his moan, not bothering to turn around, and continued his hold on Z.

Agent Caj appears, standing behind Curdur, positioning his blaster barely touching the back of his head.

AGENT CAJ. All right. Let him go.

CURDUR. *Smiling.* I think I'll take the shot instead. Heh-heh!

AGENT CAJ. *Confusion on his face.* What?

The enemy immediately aims for his kneecaps with his right boot, and Caj backs away before it makes contact. Curdur repositioned his hands and threw Z at Caj.

Agent Rahz flies in and tries to kick him in the face. The evil clone does multiple backflips and lands on the ground ten feet away. Z stands up on his own, refusing help from Caj, massaging his bruised arms.

AGENT CAJ. *He is staring at the clone.* What have you gotten yourself into now, Z man?

AGENT RAHZ. *She flies closer to Z and Caj, landing on the ground. She is watching the enemy.* Why does he look like him?

AGENT Z. *He is still massaging his bruised arms.* That's one of Mr. Anaheim's inventions.

CURDUR. Yoohoo! I hate to interrupt, but— *He fires his arm blaster.*

AGENT CQUA. No!! *He runs in front and materializes his shield.*

CURDUR. Pointless. *He laughs.*

The attack hits the shield, but the force causes the foreign agent to fall on his rear. He repositions his shield, pointing it straight up, and the attack shoots into the sky.

CURDUR. *He is looking up while smiling.* Hm. Good. *He looks at the four agents. He says to himself out loud.* And then there were four! *He smiles.*

The enemy raises his right arm again for another attack. Suddenly, a loud noise is coming from high up in the clouds. The agents look up. Curdur goes in for another attack, not looking at the approaching helicopter. He fires his arm blaster— Caj steps in front of the group.

The helicopter gets closer, and a person sticks their head out. It's Mr. Anaheim holding a remote control, and he presses a button. Curdur's body freezes, and his attack, but he can still move his eyes.

The blast fades away. Curdur's body slowly starts disintegrating. The clone looks at the group with a little grin, and his head disintegrates.

Mr. Anaheim destroyed his form using a unique remote control built as a safety precaution if something went wrong with the BIO-Beings.

The agents sigh in relief. Caj turns around, facing Agent CQua.

AGENT CAJ. Good to see you again, homeboy. *He smiles, and he extends his right hand closer to him.*

AGENT CQUA. Aye! It's you. Cajgie. Ha-ha. *He grabs his hand but decides to give him a brotherly hug.*

AGENT Z. *He stops massaging his arms.* How do you know him?

AGENT CAJ. *He looks at Z.* I was sent to recruit him. *He looks at the French agent.* You could *not* have come sooner!

AGENT CQUA. Dude. If it wasn't for Techy Andy, pfft. *He sighs.* Do you know how many miles I had to track this guy? Commander Addams notified me about this hacker dude roaming around my sector.

AGENT CAJ. Did you catch him?

AGENT CQUA. Dude? *He gives Caj a look.* You know I caught him! *He laughs.* He should be in Primous right about now. *He smiles.*

AGENT Z. Don't you mean *we* captured him?

Agent Rahz has her back facing Agent Z. She is facing the helicopter and watching Anaheim exiting the chopper and walking toward the agents. When she heard what Z said, she couldn't help herself and started smiling and blushing. She got control over her emotions quickly so that Mr. Anaheim wouldn't have gotten the wrong impression.

MR. ANAHEIM. *He approaches the female agent and stops walking.* I want to thank you all for what you did for me.

The four agents stare at him. Agent Z is excited to be this close to one of his idols finally. It is too bad he is in agent form right now.

AGENT CAJ. No problem, sir. My apologies in advance; I have to take you to our headquarters. Our boss would like a word with you about— well, you know.

AGENT Z. *He snaps back to reality.* What? We're taking someone who's not affiliated with us to our base?

AGENT CAJ. Yes, Z man. *He smiles.* Let's go, guys, teleport out. Rahz, do you mind being the last one and restoring this area?

AGENT Z. *He volunteers.* I'll do it!

AGENT CAJ. Is this okay with you?

AGENT RAHZ. *She nods her head.* Mhm.

AGENT CAJ. All right, take care of this. Oh, Z. You go back to your field trip, then meet us at HQ. *He is quiet for a few seconds.* Agents, let's return to base.

The lead agent touches Anaheim's shoulder, and they both teleport first. CQua and Rahz teleport next, individually. Agent Z materializes an Invisi-Dome, and it blankets the entire area. The area becomes cleansed, and the Invisi-Dome disappears. He teleports to the Observatory to meet up with his class. Afterward, he teleports to VLORs.

He arrives in the Geared'NReady Room and walks outside in the hall, where he greets everyone.

AGENT CAJ. Everything good, Z?

AGENT Z. Yes.

AGENT CAJ. Fall in. We're going to speak with the commander.

Caj leads everyone to the operations room.

MR. ANAHEIM. *He is looking around, admiring the facility.* Fascinating development.

Upon arrival, they all stop in front of the operations room doors, and when they open, they all walk inside. Commander Addams greets his agents and personally greets Anaheim.

CO. ADDAMS. *He shakes his hand.* It's a pleasure.

MR. ANAHEIM. Oh no, the pleasure's all mine. *Shaking his hand.* What a fine organization you're running here.

CO. ADDAMS. Much appreciated. *He places his arms behind his back. He looks at the foreign agent and smiles.* Ah, CQua. It's been a while. How's everything back home?

AGENT CQUA. *Standing up straight, smiling.* The *best*, sir!

CO. ADDAMS. Excellent. *He nods.* Report.

AGENT CQUA. *Returns a head nod.* Yes sir. *Clears his throat.* After chasing Techy Andy across the Atlantic Ocean to Hidendale Springs, Illinois, I proceeded to Hidendale Observatory— where my V-Link led me. I had to disguise myself as a student in Agent Z's class. *He laughs.* No wonder you assigned me to this task. *He maintains his laughter, then stops.* Just kidding, Z.

AGENT Z. *He sneers and shakes his head, smiling.* There he met me, sir.

AGENT CQUA. I cornered Techy Andy on the top floor, and he used one of his microchip thingies and transformed a random device into a techno monster.

Agent Z is shaking his head and smiling. Agent Caj has no expression on his face, and agent Rahz is smiling on the inside.

AGENT CQUA. Then I met— *He pointed to Z.*

CO. ADDAMS. *He nods at him.* Continue.

AGENT Z. Yes, sir. *Exhales.* That's when I left my class group and transformed. I fought the "techno-monster." *He cannot help but smile as he looks at CQua's face. He straightens up his act real fast.* After I defeated it, CQua came into the room. I mean after he threw Techy Andy into the room and caused Anaheim to freak out!

MR. ANAHEIM. *Chuckles.*

AGENTS Z and CQUA. *Speaking in unison.* That's when-- *They look at each other.*

CO. ADDAMS. One at a time, please.

AGENT CQUA. I know. Rude. *He looks at Z and winks.* Yeah. So, Techy Andy used the USB that he stole and connected it to his special laptop—

AGENT Z. —and a duplicate of *myself spawned out of thin air.*

The two agents stare at each other, half smiling. They turn to look at Addams, who has a questioning look.

CO. ADDAMS. Interesting.

MR. ANAHEIM. I'll jump in here. *He pauses for three seconds.* The creation was a BIO-Being. After "Techy Andy" shot Agent Z here with his blaster-laptop thingamajig. The USB scanned Agent Z, creating a copy.

AGENT RAHZ. How is that possible?

MR. ANAHEIM. Good question. You see, the BIO-Being can take on an individual's character trait.

AGENT CAJ. Sort of like someone who is both evil and good?

MR. ANAHEIM. Not quite, but you're close. I'm talking about different personalities.

Everyone understands what the man is talking about at this point.

CO. ADDAMS. So, how did you stop this created personality? *He looks at Z, then turns his attention to CQua.*

AGENT CQUA. *He laughs.* Man!! Sir, your answer is right there. *He points at Anaheim.*

AGENT Z. Yes, sir. He used a unique remote control and shut Curdur down.

CO. ADDAMS. Curdur?

AGENT Z. It's what he called himself.

CO. ADDAMS. I see. *He is quiet for a while, then, after a minute, he looks at Caj.* You may get started on your assignment now.

AGENT CAJ. *He nods.* Yes sir. *He walks out of the room.*

CO. ADDAMS. *He turns his attention to Z.* Can you go to The Center and meet with Angela Runn, please? She's been working on a new weapon for you.

AGENT Z. Yes, sir. *He walks out of the room.*

CO. ADDAMS. Rahz and CQua, you two stand by for right now. You guys can take a meal break while I talk privately with Mr. Anaheim.

RAHZ and CQUA. *In unison.* Yes sir. *They exit the room together but go their separate ways.*

AGENT CQUA. *He says while walking down the opposite hallway.* I'm going to swing around the Atlantic and then go find a delicious American burger to devour.

Back inside the operations room ...

MR. ANAHEIM. These are the agents of VLORs. They are a friendly group, and they are respectful.

CO. ADDAMS. *He laughs.* They're a peculiar bunch, but they get the job done. So, on to important matters. The BIO-Being project was for VLORs, correct?

MR. ANAHEIM. Correct. But I don't know now. I invested seventy-five percent into the project, but I'm taking matters into my own hands and terminating the project.

CO. ADDAMS. That might be the best decision. *He nods his head in agreement.* So, since these are digital beings, are there any safety precautions limiting their return? Like, another individual attempts to reopen the project.

MR. ANAHEIM. Every hard drive will erase its existence. No one has access to this project except for a select few. Only four others, including myself, knew about the BIO-Beings. Counting yourself and your fellow agents makes nine people now.

CO. ADDAMS. I am positive my agents want to avoid dealing with another BIO-Being.

MR. ANAHEIM. *He agrees.* Who knows? One day, the project will be remade by another with a thorough foolproof safety precaution that'll prevent any hacking attempts.

CO. ADDAMS. *Deep down, he is showing an odd expression; he does not wish the BIO-Beings to get a second go.*

Season 2, Episode 10

Rivi is lying on the beach, relaxing in his usual spot. A teenage island girl with colorful rock star hair and a rock music lover sits beside him. The two islanders speak Portuguese.

KAMALEI NAKOS. Oi. (Hi.) *Smiling.*

RIVI. Oi. (Hi.) *He raises his head.*

KAMALEI NAKOS. Você está sempre sentado aqui. (You're always sitting here.)

RIVI. Eles estão vindo para me pegar. Tu olhas. (They're coming to get me. You watch.) *He is staring out into the ocean.*

KAMALEI NAKOS. Eu me pergunto por que eles deixaram seu menino doce. (I wonder why they left their sweet boy.) *Says in English.* I hope they come for you.

RIVI. Aw. Cuidadoso. (Aw. Careful.) Acho que você gosta de mim. (I think you like me.) *He looks at her and smiles.*

KAMALEI NAKOS. irmão cuidadoso. (Careful brother.) *She bends down and hugs him. She walks away.* Eu espero que você não está lá por um longo tempo irmão. (I hope you're not there for a long time, brother.)

RIVI. Love you too, sister. *He starts to look at the water again. He looks up at the clouds. Speaks Portuguese.* Espero encontrar vocês. Onde quer que vocês são. (I hope to meet you. Wherever you are.) *He sighs and continues staring at the clouds.*

The young island boy starts seeing a person moving in the clouds.

Agent CQua is flying over New Waii Island. He circles and heads back in the same direction.

RIVI. *He stares. Speaks English.* I wish soar like that one day. It be *so* cool!

Meanwhile, on Drenden Mountain, the opposite side not facing the Observatory, the barren wilderness with lots of trees, Floral and ShaVenger are fighting Pyro and Dyro. There was an order to recruit them for VICE, but the two pyro-villains had other plans.

An hour prior

Co. Talgitx sent ShaVenger to recruit the two cross-humans. Pyro and Dyro are a few bills short for their mother's surgery, so they attempt to rob another bank and choose the bank located in Dowers City, Illinois.

After being dismissed by the VICE Commander, the young cross-humans individually teleported to that location. ShaVenger came up with the plan. They were waiting behind the building for the two flame brothers. Immediately after seeing them, the boy opened a portal under them, and they were gone. They fell through and landed on Drenden Mountain, located behind the Observatory. The fight commenced. The young cross-humans ended up on different mountain parts because one of them likes using his teleporting abilities when he fights.

Floral was doing great at the beginning against Pyro, but he heated his body and threw a fire attack at her, and she was scorched.

In the present

Floral falls, screaming in pain. ShaVenger hears the screams and hurries to her location. He appears behind Pyro, throws two punches, goes to the girl, and disapparates.

That night, Agent Z teleports into his bedroom and transforms into civilian attire. The moment he changed, the metallic band, located on the upper part of his right arm, burns for a few seconds.

ZADARION. *He starts rubbing the spot.* Man, this thing is weird! Maybe it is reacting to something. *He shakes his head.* I can't worry about this right now. *He looks out his window.* I know you're out there. *He sighs.* Where are you, Morgan?

Dave Jones arrives home via taxi from SpeedWay Rail Station, located in Valousse City, Illinois. He got off the plane at Skyyas Airport in Larouse City, Illinois, and he went to the closest SpeedWay Rail Station and boarded a train to Valousse. He got off the train, caught a taxi home, arrived at his house, paid the driver, and exited the vehicle. He carries his briefcase and luggage to the doorstep. Before he can knock on the door, his wife opens it.

Mrs. Hailie Jones throws herself at her husband, hugging him tightly. The married couple shares a moment before proceeding to go inside.

The man carries his luggage, and his wife carries his briefcase. She places it on the small living room table and walks into the kitchen, where she continues to wash the dirty dishes from the dinner tonight. Dave drops his luggage by the staircase and decides to walk into the kitchen because he heard someone playing in their high chair, and he could've sworn he heard singing. He enters, walking toward Ki'liana Jones (Kiley).

DAVE JONES. Who's this trying to sing? It can't be *my* daughter. *Talking in his baby voice.* Yes, it's youuuuuu!

KILEY JONES. Dad-dababa! *Waving her toy spoon in the air.*

He kisses his youngest on her forehead. The baby closes her eyes for a few seconds, smiling.

DAVE JONES. *He looks at his wife.* Her first words, huh? *He is smiling and teasing his wife.* One out of one is alright.

MRS. HAILIE JONES. For your information, smart guy, Ki'liana's first words were her big brother's nickname.

DAVE JONES. *He makes a pouty face for a second, and he looks disappointed at his wife's response, but then he starts laughing.* Speaking of Zada, where is my little mini-me?

MRS. HAILIE JONES. *She jokes.* He *so* does not look like you, babe. But he should be up in his room.

DAVE JONES. *He points at his wife.* I'll deal with you later. *He walks to the staircase, looks at the top floor, and raises his voice.* Zadarion!! Bring yo' little butt down here!!!!

The boy hears his father shouting and calling his name. He wonders what he might've done. He goes to see what his father wants. He makes his way to the top of the stairs and looks down. Dave could not help himself. He starts smiling as soon as he sees his son. He opens his arms wide.

Zadarion shakes his head with a smile, runs downstairs, stops in the middle of the staircase, and jumps. He lands in his father's arms, and Dave swings him around and tightens his grip. The boy tries to hug tighter but cannot match his father's strength.

DAVE JONES. *He jokes.* Bigger than an elephant! *He laughs.* I can *still* catch you without breaking my back!

ZADARION. Oh, dad. *Smiling.*

DAVE JONES. I missed you too, son.

Meanwhile, at Alec's home in Kale County, Illinois, Alec is sleeping in his bed. He seems to be dreaming peacefully but tenses up after a few minutes. He tightens his fingers around his pillow.

ALECXANDER. *He looks petrified.* No. *He turns on his back.* No. *He starts moving his head back and forth.*

The boy dreams about his mother, and he's walking down a street on Sandulay Island, searching for her.

ALECXANDER. *He whispers.* Mom. Where are you?

A few hours prior (in the dream), his mother tells him to run away while she diverts the attention of an enemy Jolt'Tweiller. The enemy seeks to annihilate young Alec and his last living relative.

The boy approaches an abandoned convenience store. The store is in mint condition but has steel plates bolted to the windows.

ALECXANDER. Where are you m– *He looks up and he looks on in horror. He drops to his knees.* M– Mom!!!!!! *He starts crying, and tears begin pouring down his face. He is now on his hands and knees. He sniffs.*

His mother's lifeless body is dangling from a traffic pole, and a word is carved into her chest and written in blood on her forehead.

The offensive word is JoOc, a mixture of two different races, the Shoc'Weillers, and the Jolt'Tweillers.

He wakes up, pulling his pillow close and lying on his left side.

ALECXANDER. Mom. *He sniffs and remembers his father.* Dad.

Monday, June 12, 2107

The following day, around 0800, Sky Deubron, Captain of HighTech City Police Force in Georgia, sent one of his soldiers to Naphilia Town, Illinois. Soldier 08 waited a few months before proceeding to the meeting spot.

The man walks inside Adlum Corporation and meets Wayne Adler outside his office.

A former scientist, now businessman, worked with experiments that could enhance the qualities of humans. Adler has only one hand, but it's tough to notice at first glance.

ADLER. Ah. You must be Detective Langler! Captain Sky just sent a follow-up e-mail telling me about our meeting. How have you been doing for the past few months?

SOL. LANGLER. Sir. I have been impatient. But I'm here to assist you.

ADLER. Where is the envelope?

SOL. LANGLER. *He reaches into his pocket, pulls out a letter, and hands it to him.*

ADLER. *He opens the letter and starts reading. While reading, he asks a question.* Have you had any trouble during your wait?

SOL. LANGLER. There have been a few distractions, and I had to avoid certain people.

ADLER. Nice. *He ignores his response, paying more attention to the letter. A message beeps on his computer for a scheduled medical appointment. He checks the time, stands, walks to his door, opens it, and starts walking down the hall.* I'll contact you.

Langler walks to the elevator.

Meanwhile, around 0800, at Centransdale High School, during the summer semester, Michel is standing by his locker talking to a female student. Zhariah walks in front of him, and she smiles while passing. The girl is making her way to her locker. On her way, she passes a bulletin board with a poster displaying Morgan's face. The sign has a phone number and an e-mail address underneath the picture.

Michel stops talking to the female student as three others reach him. He looks at the former football player and two others.

MICHEL JOHNSON. *He keeps his eyes on one but speaks to Rich.* They let you out of the detention center early. Huh, rich boy?

RICH DAVIS BLOOME. Yeah. I'm going to need you to leave Dave Mikaelson's sister alone.

UNNAMED FEMALE STUDENT. Who is he talking about, Michel?

MICHEL JOHNSON. *He looks at the girl standing next to him and then at Rich again.* Please don't play with me, Rich. *He speaks to his female friend.* Come on; we're out.

The two walk away.

MITCH CONALD. Dude! You gon' let him talk to you like that?!

RICH DAVIS BLOOME. *Smiling.* It's cool. I got that homeless punk.

The three walk down the hall. Zadarion is hiding in the chemistry lab, hanging out during his free period with Alecxander Jackson.

Meanwhile, Zhariah (Zari) is at her locker, and she is switching her books out for the next period. A girl she has never seen before stumbles behind her, dropping her books.

This girl has a unique style, wearing round, circle glasses, and her hair is in pigtails. She is wearing a pink and white headband, and it covers her forehead. She is wearing shorts (knee length) with colorful socks up to her knees, and the bottom of her shorts are baggy. There are multicolored strings tied to the bottom of her shorts, and she's wearing ballet shoes.

KATIRE LENORE. Oh, shoot! Katie, you're such a maladroit. *She looks up at the girl.* I'm so sorry. I hope you forgive me. *She smiles innocently.*

DELENA BLOOME. *She passes the two girls.* Aw, the two most awkward people in the world finally found each other. *So* cute!

MARIE MIKAELSON. Yeah! *So* cute!

ZHARIAH. *She looks at older girls and raises her voice.* You know what, Delena? Why don't you shut your face!!!!

The teenager walks closer, and Zhariah starts to ball her fists. Marie pulls her back, and the two walk down the hall. Katie is impressed by Zhariah's bravery in standing up to bullies.

KATIRE LENORE. *She watches the girls walk down the hall, then looks at Zhariah.* Thank you.

ZHARIAH. Don't worry about them. *She raises her voice.* Ever!!

KATIRE LENORE. I know, and I have you by my side now! *She smiles.* My name is Katire. That's pronounced, Ka-tee-ir. But you can call me Katie.

ZHARIAH. I'm Zhariah, but call me Zari if you want to. *She looks at the girl's books that are on the floor.* Uh, aren't you going to pick them up?

KATIE. *She places her hands on her head.* Oh no! Thank you. How absent-minded of me. *She removes her hands from her head.*

ZHARIAH. *She cannot help herself; she smiles.* It's okay, Katie. *She bends down to pick up her books.*

KATIE. Thanks. *She bends down and picks up the rest.*

The two stand. Zhariah takes a book out of her locker and closes it. She turns her head, and Katie is still standing there, watching her with an inviting smile.

ZHARIAH. Uh, the bell's about to ring. It would be best if you hurried to class before you are late.

KATIE. Um. I don't know the location of Mr. Zow's Algebra class.

ZHARIAH. You have him next?! I have him too! I'll take you! *She starts walking to class.* He's an outstanding teacher; you'll like him. He's funny!

KATIE. *She is following.* Really? *She's hugging her books close to her chest. All of a sudden, she's nervous.*

ZHARIAH. What's wrong?

KATIE. Oh, nothing. It's just that you're so lovely. I have been here since the end of the fall semester and all of the spring semester, and now it is the beginning of the summer semester, and you're the only one who noticed me. *She laughs.* I know I accidentally bumped into you by your locker, but you could have ignored me.

ZHARIAH. Is it hard for you to make friends or something?

KATIE. I think I'm a fun gal! But— I don't know. I guess people our age only pay attention to boys and makeup and models and stuff like that.

ZHARIAH. *She laughs.* Girl, I agree with you there!

KATIE. *She thinks she said something else and raises her voice.* It feels that way—. Oh? What? You said you agree with me?

ZHARIAH. Yah! *She giggles.*

KATIE. *She blushes and smiles. She speaks softly.* I never had anyone agree with me.

ZHARIAH. What did you say, Katie?

KATIE. Nothing. *She now has a big smile.*

The two arrive at Mr. Zow's Algebra class.

ZHARIAH. Let's get to our seats.

KATIE. The last one in their seat is a rotten egg! *She runs into the room and sits near the window in front of the class.*

ZHARIAH. *It seems she cannot stop smiling. She sits down next to Katie.* You're funny!

KATIE. Thanks! *Smiles.*

These two have become best friends in just a short amount of time.

Delena Bloome and her friend, Marie Mikaelson, look at Katie in disgust. Mr. Zow enters the classroom at that time, ready to begin his lesson.

Delena raises her hand, about to say something witty, but the instructor shoots her down harshly. All the students in the classroom laugh— until she hisses at them, and they immediately stop.

Katie is sitting in her chair, prepared to take notes. She is pleased inside; the same is true for her new friend.

MR. ZOW. Well, class, let's welcome our newest student. *He looks and points at the girl.* Welcome, Miss Lenore. We're glad to have you! Yes, you got here at the end of the fall semester (2106), but you're a new face to me. *Smiles.*

ZHARIAH. *She whispers to her new friend.* He's in charge of almost every sport in this school.

KATIE. *She looks at her for a quick second and then at her paper.*

The instructor starts his lesson for the day.

Meanwhile, around 0900, Andy hacks his way into the computer systems. He releases himself from his cell, poses as a guard, finds his flight backpack in a storage room, makes quick repairs, and breaks out of Primous Facility. While flying, he contacts his boss. He dials his phone number, the tablet rings, and he answers the call on his headset.

TECHY ANDY. Sir, a slight change of plans. I was unable to acquire the BIO-Being.

UNKNOWN CALLER. *He sighs on the other end.* That's disappointing news, Mr. Mathessen, and I have an alternative, and I'll notify you.

TECHY ANDY. Aye, Sir. *He hangs up the call.*

The man flies to Valousse City, Illinois. He changes into better clothes and gets coffee at the local coffee shop.

The coffeehouse has posters of Morgan Wiles, one on the entrance's window and three taped on a street light pole. He glances at the sign and then returns to reading his newspaper.

TECHY ANDY. Hm. I'm surprised the missing girl isn't in any of these sections. *He turns the page.*

Andy finishes his coffee five minutes later, places his newspaper on the table, and looks up. He spots someone familiar walking out of a department store. Andy balls up his fists and remembers the last time seeing him.

A few years ago, this man stole one of his microchips and used it to rob a bank in Melovaton City, South Carolina.

Andy pays for his coffee and follows him down the street.

The man walks into an alley and turns around, waiting for the person following him to show up. Andy walks up slowly, looking very unhappy.

MR. CASEY. Aw, cheer up kid.

TECHY ANDY. *He is angry, walking closer to the man.* You just had to steal my tech., didn't you?

MR. CASEY. Ah, let it go already. It's been two years!

TECHY ANDY. And I'll ensure it'll be the *last* time you see me again!

A horde of statistabots appears behind him.

MR. CASEY. *He smiles.* You are about to do what now?

TECHY ANDY. *He is mad and stops his attack.* Next time, sir. *He charges up his flight backpack, takes off in the air, and flies away from the alley.* At least I know where you are, old friend!

MR. CASEY. *He watches as he flies away and cracks a smile.* Heh.

The statistabots disappear.

Meanwhile, in the evening, on New Waii Island, Rivi is hiding in a tree, watching the beach in a mesmerized state of mind, looking for something until Agent Z appears on the beach.

Z and DiLusion fall out of a created portal, landing on the beach, and they are both still determining where they have landed. Z is holding his own in battle while studying the man's attacks rather than paying attention to his surroundings. Rivi is watching.

After a few minutes, the agent throws out an Invisi-Dome. Somehow, Rivi can see everything going on inside, up to the part where they go through another one of DiLusion's created portals, and both leave the area. The Invisi-Dome disappears.

An hour later, Rivi is looking down, walking through the local playground, when he bumps into an unknown man.

He's in his feelings again, getting this way every time he leaves the beach. He was very young when Krojo found him washed up on shore.

The boy turns his head and sees no one. The man is nowhere in sight. Rivi looks at the ground and sees a device. He reaches for it. The device looks like a fancy bracelet. Just then, Krojo spots Rivi. The elder is standing at the other end of the park, and he shouts his name. Rivi grips the piece of jewelry tight and runs to him.

RIVI. *He stops running and looks at Krojo. Speak Portuguese.* Olá, pai. (Hello, Father.)

KROJO. Getting good there with the languages, my son. *Chuckles. Speaks Portuguese.* Você estava na praia? (You were at the beach?)

RIVI. *Speaks Portuguese.* Sim. (Yes.) *He looks at the ground.*

KROJO. *He walks closer to him, speaking Portuguese.* Não se preocupe filho. (Don't worry, son.) *He places his hand on his head, spotting the bracelet, and speaks English.* Where'd you get that?

RIVI. *Confused, he forgot to conceal it and speaks Portuguese.* O Que? (What?)

KROJO. Speak in English, Rivi.

RIVI. Sorry, Papa. *He raises his left arm.* Do you mean funny-looking thing here?

KROJO. *He knows. Speaks Portuguese.* Venha comigo. (Come with me.)

They arrive home in less than twenty minutes. Once inside, the elder locks the doors, barricades them, and proceeds into the kitchen and spins the small, round table counter-clockwise ten degrees. The table separates, and a space opens up underneath.
KROJO. Follow me.

The boy is a little spooked, but he trusts him enough to follow him. Once they're inside, the table changes back. They are deep underground in a cave-like area. There's no secret lab or anything like that; it's a space with two boulders. Krojo takes a seat and nods to Rivi.

KROJO. *He sighs.* I didn't expect you to be selected.

RIVI. *Confused.* What you talking 'bout, Papa?

KROJO. The man who created that device you're holding goes by Cyphur McDonald.

RIVI. *He looks at the device and back at Krojo.* I d— I don't— *He's trying to speak clearly.* I don't get it.

KROJO. VLORs selected you to become a part of their organization.

RIVI. What a VLORs?

KROJO. Let me start from the beginning, from what I know. Years ago, this alien piece of technology landed on this planet, but not sure when. Four scientists were on one of the California peninsulas named Orailie Island. They tried to crack the code, but the alien piece of an unknown metal wasn't responding to our human technology. Then, from what my brother told me, the unknown foreign metal reacted. It tore up the whole lab and fled.

RIVI. It got up ran?

KROJO. It lifted off the scientist's examination table and flew straight out of the building's ceiling. *He sighs.* My brother told me that the four scientists, including himself, went their separate ways after that.

RIVI. Really?

KROJO. *He points at the device.* Strap it to your right wrist. Let's see what it can do.

RIVI. Okay. *He struggles to put it on.* Like this?

KROJO. Perfect. *He is looking at the device.* The V-Link? Where is the— Ah! Swipe three fingers across the center. There! *He pointed.*

Rivi does what Krojo says. Once he swiped three fingers, the device scanned him. His body glows for five seconds, and then he feels a pinch.

RIVI. Ouch! *He is rubbing his arm, now trying to take the device off.* Stupid medal. *(He pronounces "metal" as "medal.")*

KROJO. No, Rivi! It is bonding to you.

RIVI. It hurts. *He's scared.*

KROJO. Listen to me. *He grabs his shoulders.* You have to be strong now, which may help you find your parents. *He lets go of his shoulders and smiles.* I believe in you.

The boy's body becomes enveloped in the light emitting from the device. His clothing changes and the white light fades after five seconds. He is wearing all-white cargo-style pants with black and silver combat boots. He also has an all-white t-shirt and a communicator on his forehead.

RIVI. I feel fast, Papa. *He is beyond impressed.*

KROJO. You are fast, my little revving coyote!

RIVI. Like that name. *He smiles.*

KROJO. We should refer to you as Rev. *He smiles.*

RIVI. Agent Rev. *He laughs.*

The V-Link on the boy's right arm shoots a light at the ground five feet from him. A hologram of Commander Addams is in between them.

CO. ADDAMS. Ah. *He smiles.* Another agent has joined. Welcome aboard, Agent—?

AGENT REV. Rev! *He smiles and looks at his Papa.*

CO. ADDAMS. I can tell you're going to be a handful— but in a good way! *He smiles, and then he looks at Krojo.* My deepest apologies for what happened to your older brother, Cyphur.

KROJO. It is okay, Sir Addams. *He nods his head.* I have trained my son here in the arts. *He sighs.* My brother thought he might be a good match for VLORs.

CO. ADDAMS. We will see. *He smiles and looks at the new agent.* I will contact you when I have an assignment. Talk to you soon. *His hologram disappears.*

AGENT REV. What he mean?

KROJO. You're an agent now. A special soldier— A superhero!

AGENT REV. I love superheroes. Yes! *He is smiling.* So means I fly?

KROJO. I wouldn't try that just yet. Wait until your headset tells you how to use your arsenal.

The boy's gear dissolves back into his V-Link, and he's wearing his regular clothes.

Meanwhile, on an island in the Caribbean, Scientist Rayley Nickolson is working hard at developing his latest android.

He is a middle-aged scientist who loves building robots, which is his passion. Nickolson downloaded all the specifications, skills, abilities, and emotions into it. After three hours of tinkering with his computer, he presses the enter button on his keyboard. The android takes time to fully awake. During that time, he turns his head to look at three musical androids in their stasis pods. The android opens her eyes and starts moving her fingers and limbs. He turns his head with a smile.

RAYLEY NICKOLSON. Let's see you stand.

The android removes herself from the operating/examination table, gazing at her new titanium hands and metallic fingers. After closing her fingers, she places her arms at her sides and stares into her creator's eyes.

UNNAMED ANDROID. Why am I made of metal? I was human. What did you do to me? *Her eyes fill with artificial tears.*

RAYLEY NICKOLSON. All you need to know about your past life is that you were in a car crash. Two rival gangs in Winndow City, Illinois, were fighting. Some mystery person pulled you from a car before it exploded. I found you at Kaydale Hospital in the burned victims unit. I had you brought here to my secondary lab.

UNNAMED ANDROID. And you turned me into a cyborg.

RAYLEY NICKOLSON. An android, to be precise. Most of your internal organs are still present.

UNNAMED ANDROID. Why me? Why didn't you just let me die?

RAYLEY NICKOLSON. People who endure a tragedy deserve a second chance.

UNNAMED ANDROID. *She's quiet for a few seconds.* Do you know my name, my real name?

RAYLEY NICKOLSON. I do. I could give you the information about who you used to be, or do you wish to have a fresh start with a new name? The choice is yours.

UNNAMED ANDROID. Yes. Please.

RAYLEY NICKOLSON. *He exhales.* Shoneil Grailer.

UNNAMED ANDROID. *She looks at her newly built body.* Pfft, android huh? You should be calling me Graizoid.

RAYLEY NICKOLSON. *He laughs.* I didn't say it at first. *He stops laughing.* Listen. I have a meeting in Hidendale Springs, Illinois. Some conference I have to attend. Do you mind staying here, acting as my secretary? I peeped the credentials of your past life. You're good.

GRAIZOID. Sure, and it's not like I can go anywhere. I'll probably rust if I take a nice hot shower.

RAYLEY NICKOLSON. Thank you. I owe you one.

The man grabs his luggage by the door and a few files on his desk, placing them in a small folder. He rushes out of the lab to the stairwell, stops at the top, turns his head, and faces the door.

RAYLEY NICKOLSON. Take care, sis. *He goes downstairs, out of the building, heading to the parked taxi.*

He's making his way to the island's airport. Meanwhile, Agent Z falls through one of DiLusion's portals. The fused being's voice is taunting.

DILUSION. You will never understand what I am, little one.

AGENT Z. *He's floating inside a portal, shouting.* Why don't you take us back to Earth for a fair fight!!!!

DILUSION. Now, where's the real fun in that?

The man shows his face for a split second. The boy swings, but DiLusion's face disappears. Agent Z's body starts to feel heavy, pulling him down. He is screaming while falling through the portal.

AGENT Z. *He is shouting.* I swear I will defeat youuuuuuuuuuuu!!!!

The portal opens up below. Z sees an opening under him, falls straight through, and his body disappears. He reappears in the middle of an unknown park, and he looks around, and there is no one around.

Suddenly, two preteens run incredibly fast toward the agent's current position. Z turns his head, and the two preteens crash into him.

A young blue-haired boy stands, and then the young pink-haired girl.

DONNY. *He dusts himself off and looks at the other boy.* Hey! Watch it! *He grabs the young girl's right hand.* Let's keep moving, Sally. *He shouts.* **SwiftRun!**

AGENT Z. *He gets off the ground after looking at the two youngsters in confusion.* Who are you guys?

The young boy shouted a mysterious word and started running incredibly fast while holding onto the young female's hand. The agent shakes his head and stares into the distance.

AGENT Z. I must be losing it. That or– DiLusion's portals are affecting my mind. *He checks the virtual three-dimensional map on his V-Link, and it starts scanning the area.*

Z is checking where the enemy's portal sent him. The V-Link stops scanning, concluding he's at Bayside Park in Falarbor Bay, Montana. He teleports back to Illinois, inside VLORs, where Agent Caj greets him.

AGENT CAJ. *He's walking closer to him.* Where have you been man?

AGENT Z. *He lowers his head and then looks back up at Caj.* This dark, purple, freaky-looking alien dropped me in Montana. I was searching for Pyro and Dyro when I saw him. It's weird. His body and way of teleporting were similar to ShaVenger's. But it was different. He's calling himself, DiLusion.

AGENT CAJ. Is he about average height, and does he wear a torn lab coat?

AGENT Z. Yes! But this guy was no scientist. You must be thinking about the disappearance of Lilori Daniels – the young college professor who went missing a while back. The local news has reported his disappearance for months, and I don't think they are the same person.

AGENT CAJ. With all these cross-human appearances and this other weird stuff happening, it sounds possible.

AGENT Z. Yeah. I agree.

AGENT CAJ. You be careful out there, Z man.

Agent Caj walks past the younger agent, heading to the transport room to leave VLORs. Z goes to see Commander Addams to fill him in about this mysterious DiLusion before heading home for the day.

Z approaches the operations room. Just as he is about to go inside, CQua turns a corner and walks past him.

AGENT CQUA. Uh, Addams is speaking to some old guy who is missing his right hand. Don't ask.

AGENT Z. Thanks. *He makes his way to the Geared'NReady room.* I can meet my dad for dinner. Oh, man. I am starving! *He places his right hand on his stomach.* I wonder where we're going to take me to eat?

The boy teleports inside a restroom stall at the usual arcade he and Sam Kerry hung out. He changes into civilian attire, exits the booth while putting on his backpack, and walks to the sink to wash his hands.

ZADARION. *He walks out of the restroom and bumps into a young man.* Excuse me. *He doesn't pay attention to his face or turn around. He walks to the arcade games and kills some time by playing a few games.*

The nerdy young man is exiting the arcade.

Two hours later, Zada gets on a city bus and makes his way to MechaWaste, a garbage waste, and recycling separating facility.

Meanwhile, in San Drean on Sandulay Island, inside FropYoli Ice Cream Shop, a male Caucasian-Asian teenager wearing a long black jacket is eating ice cream.

San Drean is a beautiful place this time of year. The palm trees line the roads in a beautifully symmetrical pattern leading you to a destination. The colorful flowers on the ground are waving by the wind's gentle breezes. The sun shines bright, and everyone is outside, enjoying the lovely weather. The ice cream shop is on a quiet side street between a barbershop and a gas station.

AGENT ERON. *He spoons ice cream into his mouth and swallows.* What a well-earned break after searching for those children on God. *He licks his lips.* I've missed FropYoli! They don't have these shops in HighTech City. *He stops talking and finishes his dessert.* Mm!

Forty minutes passed in Hidendale Springs, Illinois, and the city bus dropped Zada outside the building. He walks in front of the building and up the long flight of stairs. He enters the building, and the security guard, posted by the entrance, grants him security clearance to go upstairs. His father is a corporate executive, and he works on the top floor.

The boy walks out of the elevator and approaches his father's office. He knocks first, turns the doorknob, and sticks his head into the room.

MR. ADLER. I want to say– *He turns his head to the office door as Zada peeks into the room.*

DAVE JONES. Excuse me. *He walks to his son.* Zada, wait for me outside; it won't take long.

ZADARION. Okay. *He nods his head, closes the door, and he takes a seat next to the door.*

Dave apologizes for the interruption, and he finishes a meeting.

Later that night, in Hidendale Springs, Illinois, Michel leaves his part-time job at Maxie's Bar & Grill. He crosses the street, getting close to the orphanage where he currently lives, seeing Rich is walking toward him. He has that 'up-to-something' smile on his face.

MICHEL. What's so funny, rich boy?

RICH DAVIS BLOOME. You!

He runs toward Michel. Mitch sneaks up behind Michel, holding a baseball bat, and strikes him in his back. He falls. Rich comes in, stomping him. Michel grabs his foot and twists it, and he loses his balance and falls. Michel slams his left fist into his left kneecap, and the teenager curses loudly. Mitch starts to swing the bat again, but he's punched in his no-no zone, drops the bat, and grabs his crotch as he falls. Michel stands up, but Brady tackles him and starts beating him. Michel's holding his arms out in front of his face, shielding himself, and Michel manages to grab his head, pulling him into a headlock.

Mitch and Rich stand up and kick Michel, who's on the ground with Brady on top of him. Michel changes their position. Mitch and Rich are now kicking and punching Brady. Michel manages to stand, letting go of Brady's head. Rich and Mitch pursue Michel. The three are fighting near the street.

Despite the surprise onslaught, Michel handles himself well against them.

He punches Mitch across his face and pushes him into Rich. They smack into a parked car. Brady runs up from the side and tackles him in the street. Michel stands up, wiping the blood off his lower lip. He watches Brady and the other two standing on the sidewalk. They are breathing heavily, and they're watching him.

Suddenly, a truck speeds down the street and hits Brady and Michel. Brady's struck from behind, and Michel's hit because he was standing next to him. The truck's wheels run over Brady, killing him. Michel's body flings into the air and lands on the concrete; his body is bleeding from two massive injuries. He's twitching on the pavement. The other two run away.

Someone from Michel's work walks out and sees him, and the person calls the police. An ambulance arrives moments later. Police start an investigation, first checking surveillance cameras in the area. Mitch, Rich, and the driver are sent to Gowdon's Prison within six hours, waiting for their court dates. The drunk driver for driving while intoxicated and speeding, and he will serve six years. Mitch and Rich managed to get around being charged as adults, and they're sentenced to six months of community service and then house arrest until March 2108.

Tuesday, June 13, 2107

The following day, Auntie-Mama (Abigail Johnson) and Zhariah arrive, via public transportation, at Crumarus Hospital to visit Michel. It's west of Tarainound Street, and the hospital is closer to Wayworth Bridge, leading to Ococo Town, Illinois.

A doctor tells Auntie-Mama that Michel did not make it.

Zhariah is a complete mess; tears are pouring down her face. The doctor gives his condolence and leaves to attend to his next patient.

The teen girl storms out of the hospital, bawling. Auntie-Mama chases after calling her name.

At six o'clock in Kale County, Illinois, Alecxander is sleeping in his bed, dreaming. He wakes in a place called Cloud Baria, a small city-like area, presently hiding in the clouds somewhere. The young guardian, Gai, lost his ability to sense its presence. Their home city moves as the clouds move. It has been untraceable since the Jolt'Tweillers and Shoc'Weillers fought in 2007.

For the first time, Alec sees the people of Cloud Baria. He sees Gai walking out of a temple towards a man watching over the city. Gai approaches Tundarick, and the two walk off, going inside another more enormous temple.

The boy's vision goes dark. He is now in a field with his parents, and they are running away from something.

Blue lightning strikes the ground before them, and they stop running. They turn around and see five people walking toward them. Alec's father gets in front of his family to protect them. The father yells to the mom, ordering her to take their son and run. Alec's mom hesitates, grabs her son, places him on her back, and quickly sprints away from the area using a Shoc'Weillers speed technique. The father stays behind to battle the five Jolt'Tweillers, his race of people.

The boy's vision goes dark again. He is in darkness for five seconds, and then blue sparks go off in the distance. He can see menacing eyes staring at him, and he wakes immediately in fear.

ALECXANDER. MOM!!!! *He rises from his bed.*

His breathing slows. He is sitting in his bed, starting to become calm. He lowers his head and closes his eyes for mere seconds. He sees the same eyes, with blue electricity. He opens his eyes quickly.

Meanwhile, walking down Tarainound Street until the local NH Pharmacy came into view, Zadarion is closer to Alecxander's house in Kale County. He makes a left on Rouche Avenue, a residential area, and walks to Nathom Street, another residential area.

Finally approaching the house, Zadarion notices that Tundarick (Derick) is standing outside. His eyes pointed at the sky. He's dressed in a business suit instead of his typical attire. This man gives off the impression that he doesn't like anyone. He looks at the boy, and Zadarion stands straight, making eye contact with him.

It's safe to say, Tundarick likes this type of behavior. Despite not wanting Alec to interact with Terra Firma Humans, he obeys Gai's orders, stating, "Alec deserves normalcy in his life. He's been through a lot, and I do not wish to corrupt his beginnings."

He opens the door for the boy to come inside his home. Zadarion steps inside and sees Gai standing in front of the TV in the living room.

GAI. Ah, if it isn't Agent Z. *He turns around, facing him.*

ZADARION. *He's distracted by teen appearance. You got the wrong person.* But, like, I'm sorry. Your vibe feels much older, and it's crazy because I've just met you.

GAI. Long story. I am a child now. *He raises his left arm, pointing to the stairs.* Alec is upstairs in his room.

Zadarion bows as he continues making eye contact. He raises his body and turns around to face the stairs. The stairs in front of him lead to Alec's room. He walks upstairs, and Gai watches him, then looks away.

GAI. *Smiles.* Alec has found a true friend in that one.

TUNDARICK. *He walks closer to Gai.* I'm afraid I have to disagree.

GAI. *He laughs, turns around, and starts walking to the kitchen.* You were the same to me before we were both re-born, and you still act the same.

TUNDARICK. *He followed him into the kitchen.* And I'll continue. It's my duty to you and the lost guardian spirits of Cloud Baria. *He stops in front of the stove.* I don't know why you like— no trust these Terra Firma's after what they did to our people in 2007.

GAI. Like the guardian before, they all are okay. Yes, Derick, it was a tragedy.

TUNDARICK. *He sighs.* If only that boy's father hadn't hidden feelings for one of our people, we'd be home now.

GAI. One last time Derick, hush your anger. We are still technically Terra Firma Humans.

Meanwhile, in Alec's bedroom, Zadarion looks at all the action figures and science equipment in various places around the room.

ALEC. *He's lying in bed, watching him.* Thanks again for coming to visit me, Zada.

ZADARION. *He picks up an action figure from the mantle in front of him.* Oh, no problem! *He examines a toy in his hands.* I went to visit Jayla and Kiyla when they were at the hospital. *He smiles.* Is this—

ALEC. *He laughs.* Yup! The only of the seven Tumrayos action figures in the world!

ZADARION. *He places it back down on the mantle gently.* You're so lucky; my mom tried hard to find one. *He looks at Alec.* So, are you okay with Morgan's drug?

ALEC. Now I am.

ZADARION. Yeah, I tried to find Morgan after that, but she disappeared. Her mother's worried about her.

ALEC. Does Mrs. Wiles know what her daughter did to Kiyla, Jayla, and myself?

ZADARION. I do not think so, and not even Principal Harviel knows what happened. The only rumor is that Morgan Wiles has run away.

ALEC. I hope Morgan's okay, wherever she is. *He sighs.* I hope she's not beating herself up inside.

ZADARION. As Agent Z, I'm secretly searching for her when I'm out doing my daily patrols.

ALEC. Do you mean the vigilante activity you started when Morgan went missing? *He starts smiling.*

ZADARION. *He smiles back.* No. *Shakes his head.* Anyway, don't worry, I'll find her and bring her home.

ALEC. *He sits up in his bed.* Oh, and Zada? Please don't mention to the police or Harviel what Morgan did. I know she did not mean it.

ZADARION. Yeah, sure! I know she would never do anything to hurt people, and she doesn't have an evil bone in her body. *He waits a while to ask.* So, are you ready to go back out there?

ALEC. You mean— *He punches the air in front of him two to three times.*

ZADARION. Oh, yeah! *He laughs.*

ALEC. I feel good, honestly. It's just—?

ZADARION. What?

ALEC. After I woke up, the electric field inside my body was messing up.

ZADARION. Meaning, please?

ALEC. My electrical field is all crazy now after Morgan gave me a double shot of her invented drug. I tried turning my body into electricity but nothing. It's been a few days, dude. I don't even think I can speed-run anymore.

ZADARION. Oh. *He lowers his head for a few seconds before looking at him again.* I'll help you with that! *He smiles.*

ALEC. I honestly don't know what you can do to help me. Gai and Derick don't know what's going on, and I haven't even told them the exact details yet. They have too much to worry about, and I don't want them to worry about me. I'm already a half-breed.

ZADARION. *He points at Alec.* Aha! I knew you were a cross-human!

ALEC. *He laughs.* You're not even close, dude.

ZADARION. Then what are you?

ALEC. *He hesitates. He started to speak about his true self but just shook his head.* I'll tell you some other time.

ZADARION. Ok. *He's a little disappointed by Alec's response.*

Wednesday, June 14, 2107

The next day, at Primous Facility, it is lunch hour for all inmates, including the deranged Max Gerald. This pyromaniac, and a few other inmates, are in the lunch line. Two inmates, one in the front and one in the back, try to shank him. They attack him simultaneously, but he subdues them and brutally lays them out on the floor. They're staining the tile with their blood. Four guards rush into the room and force Max onto the ground. He willingly lies down. He didn't struggle, not once. He's just laughing hysterically at the two inmates. He's dragged back to his cell.

Night falls, and all inmates are inside their cells. All guards have retired to their posts on the lower level.

There are seven floors to Primous Facility, but only three are in use. Max's cell is on the third floor, the Disordered Ward (mentally different people). The first floor is the Normality Ward (less harsh crimes). The second floor is mainly for hardened criminals (much more brutal crimes). There is word out that the remaining floors are for cross-humans.

This facility is on the east coast, close to America, and it's the only building occupying the island in the middle. Director Cordonald Miles is the man in charge. He is in his mid-thirties, has brown eyes, and is of average height. His hair is always in different colors. He likes styling his hair to look hip, and he always wears business suits to work. His job is to keep track of all the inmates, record the number to the government to get proper food funding and perform other duties.

Max is lying in his rack, with his hands behind his head. He has his eyes closed for what appears to have been five minutes and starts hearing a whisper or tinkering noise coming from downstairs.

MAX GERALD. *He opens his eyes, smiling very concernedly.* Abandonment!? *He shrugs his shoulders and lays down on his rack.*

A special squadron of troops is on Methphodollous Island, making their way inside.

One by one, an inmate falls unconscious. The squadron is shooting every inmate with special tranquilizers.

After tranquilizing all the guards and inmates, the squadron makes its way to Max's cell.

Upon arrival, one squadron member shoots metallic ion bullets at the cell doors. The ion bullets form a chain with metallic links, and the links attach to his cell, and the doors explode. Max is startled, and he stands up. He stares into the smoke and starts smiling once he sees lasers pointing at him.

The squadron points their guns at him, and he looks ready to die.

MAX GERALD. *He starts chuckling.* Is it dessert time already!? *He jokes.*

Before they can fire their weapons, Agents Z and Rahz surprise them from behind and knocks them all unconscious. Z threw an Invisi-Dome out of an open window. The Invisi-Dome blanketed all of Primous Facility. Everyone inside will not remember anything today, and Max's cell repairs itself. Rahz slaps V-Cuffs on the deranged psycho, laughing hysterically at Agent Z.

MAX GERALD. *He's excited to see him.* Agent Z! It's so good to see you again, my boy!

AGENT Z. *He is not showing any emotion.* Shut up. *He uses his V-Link to immobilize him, and he calls HQ.* Commander Addams. Agent Z is here. Do you copy?

CO. ADDAMS. *He is on his headset.* Addams speaking.

AGENT Z. Sir looks like ZEXTERN tried to assassinate Max Gerald as you predicted. *He is looking at the unconscious squadron.* This unknown group works for ZEXTERN, but I am not sure. The V-Cuffs should be sending you the information about them now. Agent Rahz and I are returning to HQ with Max Gerald. Please meet us in the interrogation room. Over and out.

The two agents teleport to HQ, escorting an immobilized Max Gerald.

Thursday, June 15, 2107

The next day, Agent Caj hides in a parking garage in Valousse City, Illinois. He's waiting for someone and knows when they'll get off work, and someone goes by Cyprian Keene, a twenty-two-year-old computer analyst for Salmante Corp. A company that deals with creating nutritional supplements and energetic awareness. The company's slogan, "The genius of non-fictitious ingredients often lies in their believability. Now you can buy a bag of our product, and without worry, you will have all your nutritional needs."

About a week ago, VLORs picked up on a signal, placing McMillan in Montana. During that week, Caj researched several businesses in the area and came across Salmante Corp. He heard about Cyprian

Keene's new job on the local news station in Montana. Cyprian has excellent skills, and VLORs has been tracking his whereabouts since his run-in with VICE a few years back. On November 2105, VICE grunts wanted him for his expertise. Agent Caj arrived at the scene and stopped them, and he used his V-Link to erase Cyprian's memory.

Earlier this week, Caj investigated Cyprian's sudden appearance in the state. He went looking for him at several community colleges that he attended. He heard on TV that he's working at Salmante Corp, the same place as Mr. McMillan.

Presently, Cyprian exits the Tuxcen Community College, walks into the parking garage, and Caj jumps him. Cyprian does not see his attacker, and he is out cold. The agent uses a ninja move to become a replica of him.

Ninja-trained Caj can use Nuaiatsu by manipulating energy using different hand and finger positions, the Ren tah Chu technique. Chakra is an energy point in the human body, and Chakra connects with Tihn to access energy channels inside the body. Tihn guides the body's energy using hand and finger positions. Chakra and Tihn, with the help of Ren tah Chu, become a unit to summon supernatural powers to the individual.

Caj accesses Keene's cellular device and discovers he has a meeting with McMillan. It's his first day on the job. He places the unconscious Cyprian inside a stasis pod, which shrinks, and he puts it inside his suit pocket. He gets inside Cyprian's vehicle and drives out of the parking garage.

A few hours later, he arrives at Skyyas Airport in Laroouse City, Illinois, with all of Cyprian's personal information and luggage (artificially "fake"). After an hour, Cyprian boards the plane heading to Lake County, Montana.

AGENT CAJ. *He is in the form of Cyprian Keene. He sighs and talks in his mind.* This Ren tah Chu technique is fantastic, but nothing beats teleporting. *Quietly to himself.* I must stay in character until the time comes. *He sits in his seat, and the plane takes off moments later.*

Meanwhile, Agent Z is walking the halls inside VLORs, waiting for his meeting with the Commander. Max Gerald is inside the secure room.

The following day

The intercom turns on, and the Commander calls Z, CQua, and Rahz into the operations room. Rahz, Z, and CQua enter the operations room five minutes later. Commander Addams enters the room ten minutes later.

CO. ADDAMS. How are my three young agents?

CQUA, RAHZ, Z. Excellent, Sir!

CO. ADDAMS. My apologies. I needed a day to get in touch with Cordonald Miles.

AGENT Z. I'm sorry, sir. Who is he?

AGENT CQUA. He's the Director of Primous. *He laughs.* How did you not know this, Z?

AGENT Z. Excuse me for missing out on a brief.

AGENT CQUA. *He stops laughing and looks at Rahz.* Did you know?

AGENT RAHZ. *She says with a straight face.* No.

CO. ADDAMS. Okay, Mr. Miles is with us to a certain extent. He doesn't have security clearance to VLORs, but he is knowledgeable about VLORs and VICE, agents, and now cross-humans.

AGENT CQUA. *He looks around the room.* Has anyone seen Caj?

CO. ADDAMS. That's part of why I needed you all here. Caj is on an assignment to investigate ZEXTERN.

59

Z and Rahz are shocked, and CQua smiles while sitting at a computer desk.

AGENT CQUA. *He is smiling, and he whispers.* Goodbyeeee ZEXTERN.

AGENT Z. *He raises his voice.* Sir! You had him go by himself?

AGENT RAHZ. Sir. I agree. Caj will die. Why would you do such a thing?

AGENT CQUA. *He shakes his head, smiling.* Do You guys not know about Caj?

AGENT Z. How can you be so calm?!

CO. ADDAMS. Z, calm down. You too, Rahz. I wouldn't have sent Caj if I knew he could not handle it.

Z turns around, tightening his fists. He is thinking about going to assist.

Meanwhile, Keene arrives at Polson Airport in Lake County, Montana. The man exits the airplane, making his way to meet a duty driver to take him to Salmante. The driver is wearing a black business suit with shades covering his eyes. The driver walks Keene to his vehicle, gets into the driver's seat, and takes off.

After an hour of driving, the two arrive at Salmante Corp. They get out of the car, and the driver walks him inside, and Sturgess McMillan is standing in the lobby.

MR. MCMILLAN. It's nice to have you on our team.

They walk to the receptionist's desk. The new employee is getting checked in and issued a personal identification badge. McMillan and Keene walk to the elevator, and McMillan shows him around.

MR. KEENE. It's all lovely and everything, but be honest with me, Sturgess. Where are the goods located? *He grins and winks his left eye.*

MR. MCMILLAN. *He looks at him questionably.* Follow me.

MR. KEENE. That's what I'm talkin' 'bout. *Part of Caj's personality slips out.*

The boss leads him into the hall again and walks to an all-white wall. There is nothing on it. This wall is unusually bare, considering other office buildings have pictures of "what not to do with your money" everywhere. The man places his right hand on a specific spot on the wall, and a space opens up. The room is dark, and there is a stairwell going down. He points inside, Keene starts walking down first, and McMillan follows behind. The space in the wall closes.

MR. KEENE. *He is thinking to himself.* Oh, this will be your final day, ZEXTERN.

MR. MCMILLAN. We're almost at your appropriate workstation.

MR. KEENE. Excellent! I cannot wait to start this fantastic job!

After ten minutes, they reach the bottom, and a door in front of them slides open. Mr. Keene is astounded by what he sees. The room is enormous, and many employees and scientists are hard at work.

MR. KEENE. What are they doing?

MR. MCMILLAN. They're collecting progress on what the scientists have achieved so far. *He slaps his shoulder.* Come this way. *He points across the room at the elevator.* Your workstation is on a higher floor.

MR. KEENE. Sweet!

They walk past many hardworking employees, finally making it inside the elevator. McMillan presses the eighth-floor button, and the doors close.

MR. MCMILLAN. *His cellular rings, and he answers his phone. He speaks low.* Hello there, Dex. *He pauses.* Yes. I have it in my office. Let me drop off the newest employee at his workstation. I will call you once I'm in my office. *He waits on the phone for five seconds before he hangs up.*

The elevator stops on the eighth floor, and the two exit. McMillan walks Keene to his workstation. When they arrive at his workspace, he gives him the card key, and Keene takes it and swipes it vertically into the slot. The door opens, and the two walk inside.

MR. KEENE. *He looks around the office and walks closer to his desk, admiring his new office.* Thank you for hiring me. I promise to deliver 100% as long as I'm here! *He extends his right hand.*

MR. MCMILLAN. *He shakes his hand.* You're welcome. Now, get to work. *He lets go of his hand and walks out of the office.*

The employee watches as he shuts the office door. He focuses his ears on the elevator, which beeps, and Mr. McMillan steps inside. The doors close.

MR. KEENE. *He sighs and loosens his tie.* Stuck up, ass! *He raises his index, middle, and ring finger above his head. He twists his right wrist three times, sideways and down once. His V-Link becomes visible.* Okay, let's get to it. *He walks to the desk and uses his V-Link to access the database.* And the Lord said, Let there be'ith a miracle!!

Caj accesses all of ZEXTERN's archives into his V-Link, then logs out of the computer. He points his index and middle finger (right arm) out in front of him. He twists his wrist to the left once, then raises his right arm in the air. His V-Link disappears, including his whole body.

MR. KEENE. *He loosens his tie a little.* I swear. I don't understand why people choose to wear suits. *He walks to the door.* It's time to say goodbye, ZEXTERN. *He walks out of the office, making his way down the hall.*

An employee is walking down the other hall. Mr. Keene, invisible at the moment, approaches the side of the left wall cautiously. He stops at the end of the hall, waiting for the employee.

Five seconds later, Mr. Keene quickly reaches out for the man's swinging arm and flips him onto the floor. He punches him in the chest, and the employee is unconscious.

MR. KEENE. Well, that's one. *He peeks down the other hall, sees no one, and materializes a V-Veil.*

Once attached to a person, a small, dime-sized coin turns them invisible. If the person is unconscious, they will remain that way as long as the device is in place or whoever activated the technology is nearby.

Mr. Keene attaches the device to the employee as if it were a badge and pins it on his chest. He is invisible now and lying close to the wall. Keene makes his way down the other hall.

MR KEENE. *He raises his V-Link closer to his face and checks the building's blueprints.* I am on– *He pauses.* –the eighth floor, and McMillan's office is there. *He points to the tenth floor on the digital map. He lowers his V-Link.* Since I already downloaded

ZEXTERN's database, I'll have a little fun now. *He cracks his knuckles.*

He runs down the hall on the eighth floor, enters every work center, knocks out every last person, and places V-Veils on their bodies.

After ten minutes, he is now on the ninth floor, hiding in an unoccupied laboratory. He successfully took care of every employee and changed back, deciding it was no point in remaining as Cyprian Keene. The invisibility wears off as well.

AGENT CAJ. Yeah, that's better. *He massages his wrists.* Okay. Only one floor left, and the tenth floor is "the final boss." *He smiles.* It was a good decision to leave the stasis pod with the real Keene inside his vehicle at Skyyas Airport. Within a few hours, the stasis pod will disappear, and he'll wake with no memory of ever accepting a job here.

Suddenly, alarms sound throughout the building. Caj has a stupid grin on his face.

AGENT CAJ. I completely forgot to disable the security alarm. *He laughs. He spots several employees running toward him.* Come on. *He smiles.*

He runs to the employees and engages in combat, punching three ZEXTERN employees and dodging punches from five others. He's shoved to a wall, but he grabs the employee's arm, twists it, knees the employee in the face, and flips him on the floor.

Meanwhile, Agent Z is at VLORs, trying his hardest to pinpoint Caj's signal using his V-Link.

AGENT Z. Nothing is showing up. *He groans.* Ah! Come on, you stupid—. *The device pinpoints Caj's signal, and he smiles.* Yes! *He says excitedly and teleports to Salmante Corp.*

Rahz is peeking from inside the Geared'NReady room. She was secretly watching him trying to find a way to go and assist Caj.

Meanwhile, Z appears on the first floor at Salmante Corp and feels a searing, burning pain going down his right arm.

AGENT Z. Ah. *He starts rubbing his arm.* Focus, Z. You have to help Caj. *He tries his hardest to ignore the pain and makes his way to the top floor.*

Meanwhile, Caj is battling ZEXTERN employees on the tenth floor, and he does a one-arm cartwheel, kicking two in their heads.

AGENT CAJ. Ha! I miss these assignments! *He is smiling and sees a person coming from the corner of his left eye.*

UNNAMED EMPLOYEE. I'll wipe that smile off your face! *He swings his fist.*

AGENT CAJ. *He catches the employee's arm, kicks him in his chest, and flips him on the floor.* Okay, this is starting to get old. *He rushes at the remaining ZEXTERN employees and knocks them all to the floor. He flips over one remaining, kicks him in his head, and lands on the floor. He watches the employees struggling to stand.* I guess that's all they got in them. *He whispers—*Boss man. I'm coming for you. *He walks quickly to McMillan's office and stops at the door.*

MR. MCMILLAN. *His voice echoes throughout the building.* You Neanderthal! Do you think your fictitious disguise of Cyprian Keene fooled me?

AGENT CAJ. *He laughs.* I was counting on it!

MR. MCMILLAN. Why don't you step into my office, and we can see who the better man is?

AGENT CAJ. *He smiles.* Oh! You're just reading my mind. *He opens the office door.*

It's almost empty, and the only thing inside is a desk and a computer, and there is no other furniture.

AGENT CAJ. *He balls up his fists and looks up at the ceiling.* Nice. I see you're a fan of running.

MR. MCMILLAN. Oh, not quite. Why don't you look at the computer?

The agent walks over to the computer and looks at the screen. He sees Agent Z chained to a wall with several ZEXTERN employees standing next to him. McMillan walks in front of the camera, revealing himself. Caj has a smile on his face.

MR. MCMILLAN. *He is not looking too happy.* I found this young man not long ago, and I say he came looking for you by his attire.

AGENT CAJ. Not quite bright, are you, McMillan?

MR. MCMILLAN. Excuse me?

AGENT CAJ. So yeah. *He starts pacing in the office while looking at McMillan's face on the computer.* Here is a bit of a lesson for you. *He positions both arms in front of him, and his body turns to dust.*

MR. MCMILLAN. *His jaw drops.*

AGENT CAJ. *He is standing behind McMillan.* You see, Boss man. It would be best if you never underestimated a ninja.

MR. MCMILLAN. How'd you—? *He has a look of fear in his eyes.*

The employees standing by Agent Z attack, and Caj defeats all of them, then turns to face McMillan. He throws something small behind his back at Z, and the chains holding him to the wall rust and fall to pieces.

AGENT CAJ. It would be best if you did your homework.

MR. MCMILLAN. *He is furious but in a state of confusion.* You will not stop me. *He shouts.* ZEXTERN will not go down!

AGENT CAJ. On the contrary, the place was in danger when you walked me into Salmante Corp. Or, should I say, ZEXTERN HQ?

MR. MCMILLAN. No. No. Nooooo! *He pulls two things out of his pocket, holding a detonator in one hand and a mysterious vial in the other hand.*

AGENT Z. *He runs closer to McMillan but is stopped by Caj's right arm.* No! He will blow up all the evidence and us along with it!

AGENT CAJ. *He is keeping his eyes on McMillan.* No, he's not. Another thing I forgot to mention. After being escorted through ZEXTERN HQ, my V-Link- *He raises his right arm.* —disabled all active technology, embedding a virus throughout this entire place.

MR. MCMILLAN. *He cannot believe what he hears, and this cannot be. He says in a low voice.* ZEXTERN no more? So quickly. What a— *He starts breathing faster than usual.*

AGENT CAJ. It would help if you gave up—no reason to prolong this any longer.

MR. MCMILLAN. *He is gritting his teeth and eyeing Caj with a distasteful look.* ZEXTERN will live. *He drops the detonator on the floor and charges at Caj.*

Agent Z growls and gets ready to fight. Caj pushes Z a little bit so he is out of the way and prepares to fight. The man swings his free hand, and Caj leans back to dodge. McMillan jumps, and he starts kicking at Caj repeatedly. The agent slaps his legs down and then punches him in the chest. He falls on the floor, landing on his back. The other agent watching is impressed.

MR. MCMILLAN. *He is breathing unnaturally.* I— will— I— promise— *He reveals the vial in his other hand and quickly breaks it open over his mouth, drinking the contents inside.*

AGENTS CAJ and Z. *They scream out at the same time.* No!!!!

Mr. Sturgess McMillan drank a liquid created from crushed cyanide pills. He fidgets on the floor for a few seconds and then lies motionless.

AGENT Z. He— He— *He has a scared look on his face.*

AGENT CAJ. *He quickly grabs the boy's arms. He shouts.* Z! Calm down. Breathe!

AGENT Z. *Breathes in and out slowly.*

AGENT CAJ. *He removes his hands from Z's arms. He looks at the body.* It didn't have to go down like this. *He shakes his head and looks at the floor. He lifts his head two seconds later.* Now he just made my job more difficult. *He turns his head to look at Z.* I want you to teleport to VLORs and tell Addams I will be there soon.

AGENT Z. Wh— whoa! What are you going to do?

AGENT CAJ. I have to clear everything associated with ZEXTERN and make this place look like a legit Salmante Corp. Go now, Z!

AGENT Z. *He nods.* Ah, okay. *He teleports out of the room.*

Agent Caj arrives at VLORs HQ one hour later. He walks into the operations room and greets the three young agents and Commander Addams.

CO. ADDAMS. It has been a long day for you.

AGENT CAJ. Oh yeah! *He walks closer to an operator, and the person scans his V-Link.*

CO. ADDAMS. Are you ready to give your report?

AGENT CAJ. Yes, sir! *He looks around the room and locates the TV remote clicker.* Z, can you grab that for me? *He points to the device sitting on the table next to him.*

AGENT Z. Oh, sure! *He turns around, grabs the remote clicker, tosses it to Caj, and leans on the small table again.*

AGENT CAJ. *He catches it in his right hand, points it at the TV, and turns it on.* Well, Commander– after infiltrating and defeating ZEXTERN, I successfully wiped all their hard drives, and no one will ever know of their existence. I have it on my V-Link, which the operator here— *points behind him* —has downloaded into our database. But first, view this report of the news station in the area.

Everyone in the room, besides the few operators, watches the TV. A young man reports about Salmante Corp and the death of their CEO, Sturgess McMillan.

UNNAMED NEWS REPORTER. —Due to the rising customer complaints, Salmante Corp filed for bankruptcy earlier today. Judges declared the company to be, Lacking Uniqueness and Value. Sturgess McMillan, the CEO, took his own life because of drug addiction. *He whispers, but the cameras still catch it.* It sounds like this guy should meet my ex-wife. *His voice goes higher, and he continues reading the teleprompter.* Salmante Corp will be under new ownership in the weeks ahead!

AGENT Z. *He has his arms crossed.* Couldn't you come up with a better story?

AGENT CAJ. Nope. *He chuckles.*

CO. ADDAMS. An odd story to make up, but it'll do! So, what have you concluded about this ZEXTERN?

AGENT CAJ. Yes! *He uses the remote clicker to switch the TV to its PowerPoint application. He clears his throat.* Ahem. ZEXTERN, also known as **Z**est **E**xtremities of **X**enophobia and **T**echnicalities **E**nquiring **R**eliable **N**onchalant.

AGENT Z. Sure didn't think whoever created that name.

AGENT CAJ. Right? My God, what a mouthful. *Shakes his head.* So, this organization deals with finding threats of all kinds. Whatever is abnormal, operatives of this organization were to find out the cause no matter what.

As you already know, ZEXTERN hired this maniac, Max Gerald, to assassinate several enemies. Once put into custody, the organization wanted him dead, so they put a hit out on him. *He points to Z.* Agent Z here did a marvelous job looking after the immobilized maniac while I was impersonating Cyprian Keene. *He looks at Z.* Next time, he *remains* here! *He laughs and turns his head, looking at Commander Addams.*

AGENT Z. I didn't know!

AGENT CAJ. *He chuckles and straightens his act, continuing to speak to Addams.* Survivors and former employees of ZEXTERN are in jails across the country. You know, to keep them separated. Unfortunately, Sturgess McMillan committed suicide via a cyanide pill. Kudos to him for staying extremely loyal to his organization. *He pauses for five seconds.* Sir, I noticed another thing included in their database. *He points the remote clicker at the TV, and the screen goes to the next slide.* This man's face was plastered all over McMillan's office. I found little about him. ZEXTERN has been targeting Mr. Kelo Ritz for a while. I have never heard about this man or what he does. But it says in a file I downloaded as well that he is a scientist specializing in genetic mutations.

AGENT CQUA. Some freakaweirdo scientists are experimenting with gene splicing.

Agents Z and Rahz exchange looks.

CO. ADDAMS. Well, this is excellent, Caj. Thank you— Thank all of you! ZEXTERN is no more, but that does not mean we're out of the woods. We will continue to be on the lookout for any hidden organization that may be out there. As for this "Kelo Ritz,"— We'll put this guy on our list.

Caj turns off the TV and places the remote clicker behind the workstation desk.

CO. ADDAMS. *He looks at Z.* It's time to get Max Gerald back to Primous.

AGENT Z. Aye, aye, sir! *He turns around, walks out of the operations room, and makes his way to the holding room.*

Z opens the doors and notices an unusual smile on the man's face. He's fully immobilized, yet his facial expression would make you believe he is conscious. The young agent touches the V-Cuffs and teleports himself and the immobilized criminal to the front gates of the facility.

Two guards walk toward Z and grab hold of the immobilized prisoner. Z and the two guards carry him inside and up to his original cell. Z taps a button on his V-Link, and the inmate wakes up, but he still cannot move. He has the usual creepy smile. The guards and Z are paying no attention to him. They have only one thing on their minds, to get him back to his cell as quickly as possible.

They approach the cell. Z watches the two guards place him inside, and they walk out. The boy swipes three fingers across his V-Link, and the V-Cuffs detach themselves and disappear.

MAX GERALD. *He turns around, looking at Z.* What a disgraceful little field trip, wouldn't you agree? *He shakes his head in disappointment.*

AGENT Z. *He has an attitude.* Shuuuut up, you lunatic!

MAX GERALD. *He throws his hands in the air, turns his body, and faces his bed.* Fineee. Heh-heh. *He lies down on his bed, lying on his back. He places his hands behind his head and closes his eyes.* If that's what you want.

Agent Z and the two guards walk away from his cell, and the doors close.

MAX GERALD. *While his eyes are closed.* Oh— and Z. Be a pal and—

AGENT Z. *He is starting to become annoyed.* What! What do you want now, loser?!

MAX GERALD. *He still has his eyes closed and grins at how Z is talking.* Don't forget to say bye when you die.

AGENT Z. *He walks to the cell, placing his left hand around one of the cell bars.* What was that?

Two seconds later, one corner of Max's cell explodes. The agent is blown backward off the third level and falls on his face on the ground floor, and he's protected thanks to his suit.

Suddenly, smoke quickly fills all spaces on the facility's lower level. Z is breathing rapidly, and he's a little terrified. He can hear faint laughter in the distance. Someone is getting away, but he cannot pinpoint their position to capture the person. Z's hearing has just gone mute. There is a tiny ringing sound in his ears. More guards storm into the building, making their way to where the bomb went off. The guards put regular handcuffs on the few inmates who escaped from their cells due to the explosion.

The pyromaniac is at the top level of Primous and finds the Director's helicopter. He forces the bouncing thief, Pogo, to go ahead of him. They make it to the chopper, and it takes off. Several guards arrive at the top level via the stairwell and fire their guns at the helicopter, but it is no point. Agent Z is standing outside on the ground, looking at the sky. His hearing has gotten a little better.

AGENT Z. *He shakes his head, sighs, and fully regains his hearing. He calls his commanding officer.* Agent Z to Commander Addams.

CO. ADDAMS. You have reached him. Report.

AGENT Z. Uh, Sir. I'm sorry, but Max had a bomb inside his cell, just waiting to go off upon returning to Primous. I will do my *best* to get him back! I swear!

CO. ADDAMS. That's terrible news, Z. And yes, this is on you, so do what you must to bring him back.

AGENT Z. Yes, sir.

They both hang up simultaneously, and Agent Z teleports to VLORs.

Season 2, Episode 11

Friday, June 16, 2107

The next day, twenty miles from Hidendale Springs, Illinois, deep in VeVideer Forest, two knights are training. A young child swings his sword at a much older man in a full suit of armor, and he uses his weapon to deflect it. The man turns, throws his sword down, and the boy raises his sword to block the incoming attack. The adult warrior's sword makes contact, pushing the child backward and smacking into the tree behind him. The man points his sword an inch away from his chest, lowers it after a few seconds, and sheathes his weapon. The boy does the same and then looks at the ground, disappointed. The adult taps his right shoulder, signaling it's time to leave. They walk away, going deeper into the forest.

The two are wearing knight armor in an age in history. The adult knight's armor has battle damage, and the young knight's armor looks like cosplay. Their helmets have at least one horn protruding from the top, with black visors of different styles.

Meanwhile, Agent Z is in Dowers City, Illinois, ready to stop Chesmabite and Floral. Commander Talgitx has teleported to the scene to speak with the young agent.

AGENT Z. Finally! We get to see your face.

CO. TALGITX. And I get to see yours, my young friend.

AGENT Z. Pfft. *He tightens his fists.*

CO. TALGITX. *His right fist is holding his left fist behind his back.* Tell me. *He stops walking and looks at him.* How's that alien artifact?

AGENT Z. What?

CO. TALGITX. Oh. My apologies. You can refer to it as a superhero-styled armband.

AGENT Z. I knew what you meant. *He shouted.* Just for the record, it's mine now! You want it. *He materializes his blade.* Come and get it. *He gets in a defensive posture.*

CO. TALGITX. So be it. *He teleports away.*

AGENT Z. *He shouts.* Coward!!!!

Suddenly, Shocker appears and pushes Floral out of the way before she can summon vines to hit Agent Z.

AGENT Z. Thanks. I owe you. *He materializes an Invisi-Dome and stares at the icy villain.*

Chesmabite, one of Dr. Mache's newly activated robots, resembles an average-sized man and looks like an icicle. It has blue artificial skin.

Floral assists the android, ensuring Shocker doesn't interfere. She's using her Chlorokinesis against him.

Vines are constantly emerging from under his feet, shooting straight up, and they surround him. He cannot fully access his electrical powers, so he's flipping out of the way to evade the vines. Eventually, some of the vines wrap around Shocker's wrists and begin to tighten. He tries to break free and tries as hard as he can, but he cannot summon out any electricity.

CHESMABITE. *He's sending his robotic fists to attack the agent. He says in a robotic voice.* Run... Run... Agent.

AGENT Z. *While dodging his fists.* Shocker!! *He's worried because he is unable to access his abilities.*

SHOCKER. I'm— fine. *He's struggling to break free from the vines.*

Z sprints closer to Floral's position and jumps high into the air. His V-Link triggers his boots to switch to glide mode, and he glides in the air. Chesmabite's fists almost hit Floral, and she dives onto the ground at the last second. She quickly gets to her feet and raises more vines, telepathically ordering them to tighten around Shocker's wrists, and he screams in pain.

FLORAL. You will pay for sending my father away, agent!

The girl raises her left arm high, and a thick vine shoots out of the ground, striking Z and knocking him out of the sky. Chesmabite's fists attack him; he's punched in the face and in the chest, and the fists reconnect with his body.

AGENT Z. *He struggles to get off the ground.* So, that's how it's going to be. *He grins.*

FLORAL. *Screams.* Finish him off, Chesmabite!! *While telepathically tightening her vines grip on the other boy.*

Shocker screams out again. Z quickly materializes his blade and throws it. It acts like a boomerang and strikes the vines around Shocker. Floral's eyes follow the weapon. The vines become scratched, but the blade does not cut through them. Shocker manages to move a little. Z glides to Floral, whose head is turned away at the moment, and he grabs both hands. She turns her head around slowly and tries pulling away, but it's hopeless.

FLORAL. *She is trying to escape from Z's grip. She yells out.* Chesmabite!! *She's scared of what Z might do to her.*

The icy android sends his flying fists to attack him. Z lets go of the girl's hands and flips to his right side. His V-Link calls his blade back into his left hand, and he goes after the flying fists, even though they are now coming back at him. While Z tries to strike the flying fists, Shocker gets free and stands behind her. She's massaging her wrists.

SHOCKER. *He whistles.* Yoo-hoo. *He's smiling. He is standing behind her.*

FLORAL. *She stops massaging her wrists, looking straight out in front of her, and screams, and then many vines shoot out of the ground.*

At the same time, Shocker positions his hands out in front of him and shoots her in the back with a gust of wind, trying to summon electricity. The boy is knocked twenty feet backward by a vine and falls on his back, and the girl is blasted forward and smacks into a tree. They struggle to stand. Floral is hurt more than Shocker, but her anger forces her to continue.

Z manages to slice one of the metallic fists; Chesmabite pulls his arms back, causing the fists to return to his body. The icy creation glides closer to where Floral is standing.

CHESMABITE. *He is now standing beside the girl.* It's time for a hasty retreat.

FLORAL. *Panting.* You're right. *She closes her eyes.*

After five seconds, she throws her hands out in front of her, and many leaves surround them, and the two disappear. The leaves disperse and the two are nowhere to be found. The agent glides closer to Shocker.

AGENT Z. You good, bro?

SHOCKER. Yeah. *He's confused.* Uh Z, I thought with this Invisi-Dome in place, criminals could not escape. How did she do it?

AGENT Z. It's her V-Link. ShaVenger has one too, but he doesn't have the component to do that. Floral's V-Link works with her abilities. Another agent told me how that works, which is confusing. *He laughs.*

SHOCKER. Good luck with her. *He laughs.*

AGENT Z. All right. I'm about to release the Invisi-Dome. I know you cannot use electricity right now. Are you ready, bro?

SHOCKER. Yeah, and I have a way to avoid being detected by VLORs. *He gives Z a thumbs up.*

He releases the dome barrier. Shocker runs as fast as possible and climbs the nearest building. He does many flips and disappears into the distance. He's been feeling better and doesn't need rest anymore; lately, he has been trying to recharge himself via electrical wires or electric fuse boxes, but nothing has worked. Agent Z teleports away from the area.

Saturday, June 17, 2107

Inside a locked and unknown room inside VICE HQ, a mysterious person finally awakens from his fourteen-year slumber. The Hyperbolic Sleep Chamber releases the man.

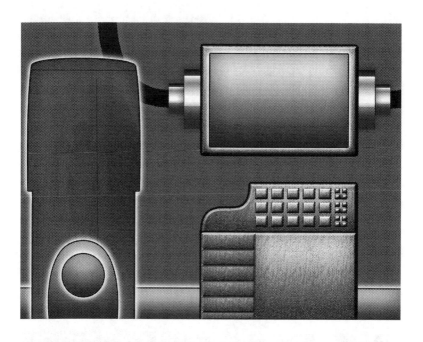

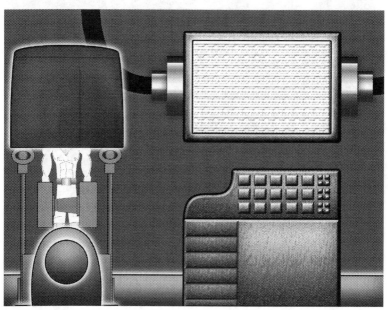

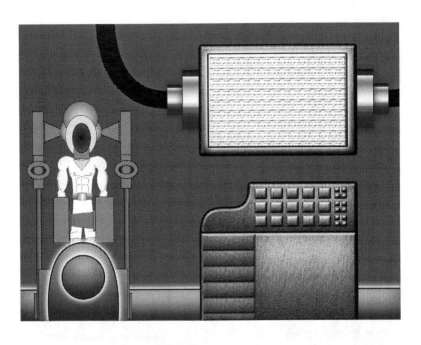

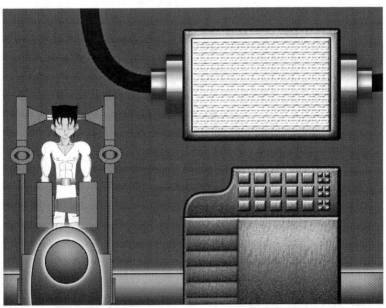

The man steps out of the machine.

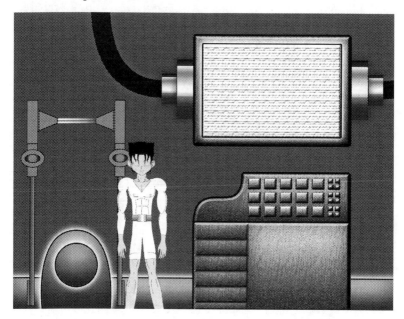

The man looks around the room. A thin TV screen lowers from the ceiling and turns itself on. A silhouetted face is on the screen. The man walks over to the thin television screen.

MAN ON SCREEN. *His voice sounds a bit distorted. It's impossible to tell the identity.* Hello, my son. It's been fourteen years since you were in that coma. I placed you here with hopes that you'll one day awaken. I am glad I did not believe the inevitable that the alien device had killed you in that room that I placed you in while I ran my experiments with my team on Orailie Island. I believe it was my fault – my experimenting with that alien device. *Static on screen.* This experiment had catastrophic results that I did not foresee happening. *Static on screen.* What's important now is that you're alive. *He sighs.* Xavier, you're currently inside an agency known as VICE. A Mario Vega has hidden its whereabouts. You'll meet him eventually. VLORs, the other half of VLORICE, is hidden as well. But Mario Vega is considered

VICE's leading engineer. He's the heart of VLORICE. I doubt he knows VLORs split from VICE. *Static on screen.* – prepared you to be a commander of VICE, to conduct order over a team of scientists. VICE is unknown to the world, and so is VLORs. We help prevent extremities around the globe. *He pauses.* So, my son, please pay attention to the rest of this recording; you'll feel at home as Commander Xavier.

The mystery man continues to watch the recording in its entirety. The thirty-two-year-old man still looks young in the face and body. He has short black hair and is of average height and toned. It is weird because he was inside the Hyperbolic Sleep Chamber for years with no exercise.

Four hours later, the man locates a suit in the hidden room and changes. He exits the room and wanders the hallway. He accidentally unleashes a horde of statistabots and neutralizes them without even breaking a sweat. He continues walking through HQ.

Meanwhile, Pyro and Dyro are back to their usual crimes, trying to get enough money for their mom's surgery. They reach their goal, but unfortunately, their mother, Mrs. Amelia Daggerton, dies. Police find their hideout in Dowers City, Illinois, and a chase ensues.

They run down Quail Street. After thirty minutes of running from the police and a small U.S. Special Forces unit, they make their way into the nearest alley. Pyro sees no hope of escaping, so he makes the ultimate decision.

While running in the alley, trying to get away from the Dowers City police and the U.S. Special Forces unit, he pushes his little brother into a brick wall. Dyro hits the brick wall, falls on the ground, and is unconscious. Pyro buries him in bags of trash in the alley. After securely hiding him, he continues running down the path until he reaches the sidewalk. Pyro is now standing across from NH Pharmacy. He stops running because he notices that the Dowers City police and the Special Forces Unit have the street blocked. The DC police are on one side, and the Special Forces Unit is on the other side. They all wear protective gear and equipment to prevent severe injuries from the flame brother's fire abilities.

Pyro's whole body ignites in flames, and he charges at the Special Forces unit. He battles them and manages to knock a few down.

After five minutes, his abilities seem to be no more. A DC policeman slaps handcuffs on him. A U.S. military officer, Caj incognito, takes over and has Pyro taken to Primous Facility. The Special Forces team continued to search for Dyro. The DC police leave the area.

Five hours later, Dyro awakens covered in filthy garbage. He crawls out of the pile of trash, pulls pieces of disgusting trash off himself, and suddenly remembers why he was running. He runs out of the alley and reaches the sidewalk across from NH Pharmacy.

DYRO. Why did you do it, brother? *He suspects Pyro got himself captured intentionally.*

Sunday, June 18, 2107

The next day, the man goes to several jails. He is persistent in breaking his brother out of prison, wherever that might be. He hides on a ferry and ends up on an island within a few hours. He walks his way to the front doors of Primous Facility.

Darius (Dyro) walks to the receptionist's office in a cunning disguise. He is posing as a young businessman, seeking entry to visit a friend.

A guard stationed at the receptionist's counter tells him that Pesto've Daggerton (Pyro) died a few hours after being brought to Primous. Darius figured scientists wanted to know how his brother had fire abilities, and the experiments must've been too much for him. Even though he thought about the inevitable, he knew his brother, and it'd take a lot to bring him down.

He exits the facility. Once close to the beach, he hears sirens from the facility and sees helicopters coming. Darius immediately runs to the ferry and throws a fireball at the coxswain, who falls overboard. Dyro hops into the small boat and drives the boat away. The man managed to dodge the authorities. Deep down, Darius wants to go back and murder the receptionist, but this would get him caught and possibly killed.

Three hours later, he makes it to Meliftorra Docks in Cauitry Town, Michigan. He runs about twenty blocks, successfully evading every person he sees.

Cauitry Town is a quiet place to live. There is no crime.

As soon as he knew it was safe, he decided to do his research, even breaking into a security room to search for Pestove's files. He breaks into Delmont's Bank, hacking the servers using their computers. He masks his online presence, stopping anyone from tracking the server he's currently using.

After a few hours of searching on the computer, he discovers that Pesto've's records are nowhere on the web, and it's like he does not exist. Darius becomes angry and leaves, never returning to Hidendale Springs, Dowers City, or anywhere near Illinois again. He lost his sickly mother and his brother. Darius had to dip before those child agents were to pinpoint his position somehow. But he had one last thing to do before he could leave. He collected most of the money he and his brother stole from banks and jewelry stores. Darius went to several areas, in Dowers City and Kale County, where he and his brother hid most of the money.

After successfully collecting the stash of loot, Darius makes himself a ghost, never to return.

Monday, June 19, 2107

Floral is in the operations room at VICE HQ and waits patiently in the center of the room.

Cameron Casey is sitting at one of the stations, looking over the surveillance equipment, and he's pinpointing coordinates for an unknown assignment.

Due to the rise of statistabots, there are no more service operators and VICE grunts. The members include Talgitx, Cameron Casey (even though he comes and goes), Dr. Machenist, ShaVenger, Floral, including the secret Mario Vega. VICE Commander Talgitx likes to keep things small; it is better to operate.

The commander gives Floral an order to investigate VeVideer Forest. She doesn't bother asking why; she's very respectable and obedient. Floral nods to her commanding officer and exits the room. She makes her way down the long hallway to the transport center. On her way there, she passes ShaVenger.

SHAVENGER. *He is leaning on the door outside of his quarters.* Where are you going?

FLORAL. *She is passing ShaVenger. She doesn't bother turning her head to look at him.* Somewhere you would not *dare* to follow me. Bye!

SHAVENGER. Yeah, whatever. *He gets off the wall and walks down the halls opposite direction.*

Floral makes it to the transport center and activates her special V-Link.

Mr. Mache developed a special V-Link, with special functions, exclusively for Floral. Since ShaVenger used to be a VLORs agent, he got his repaired after he left VLORs and updated at the same time Floral got her V-Link.

Floral teleports to VeVideer Forest and starts looking in every direction, gripping her V-Link tightly. She spots a pretty, odd-looking dandelion and uses her chlorokinesis to extend the plants around it; then, she makes the dandelion grow seven feet tall.

FLORAL. *She giggles.* Flowers are *so* beauteous! *She's smiling.*

Suddenly, she hears a strange noise and turns slightly to the left. Floral cautiously looks around the area; she's moving only her eyes. The girl slows her breathing as Mr. Casey taught her to do when trying to be as quiet as a ninja. She positions her left hand like she's ready to swipe her V-Link at any moment.

Meanwhile, at VICE HQ, Talgitx walks to his office. When he steps inside, he senses someone else but immediately walks to his wine collection for a drink. Talgitx needs to have his daily drink for the day, and he only bothers looking around his office after he drinks.

CO. TALGITX. *He has his back turned, facing his wine collection. He looks at the wall in front of him, speaking to the person behind him.* You're lost, my friend. Before I finish my drink, I suggest you leave my office. *He sips his drink once more.*

A middle-aged man sits in his chair, watching him drinking his wine. Talgitx finishes his drink, places the glass on the small table before he turn around to get a visual of this intruder. He sees a young man with black hair cut very short, wearing a suit like what he is wearing. Talgitx starts to think that this is the mysterious Informant.

CO. TALGITX. Informant?

The man continues to look at Talgitx, studying him. After a minute, he laughs and stands up, placing his hands in his pockets.

CO. TALGITX. What is so darn funny?

??????. He takes his hands out of his pockets, walks from behind the desk, and gets within three steps distance of him. Commander Talgitx?

CO. TALGITX. *He has a strange feeling about this guy.* Why are you here?

??????. He starts grinning. I'm Commander Xavier of VICE HQ. *He stops and now has a straight face.* Who might you be, friend?

CO. TALGITX. *He looks at him for a while before laughing. He walks past Xavier to his desk.* You are one delusional individual. *He continues laughing, turns around, leans on his desk, and stops laughing.*

XAVIER. *He turns his body, facing Talgitx.* Commander.

Commander Talgitx is trying to read him, but Xavier's hard to read. Talgitx is good at picking up what others think but cannot with him.

XAVIER. *He takes two steps closer to Talgitx.* Commander. *He is placing his hands in his pockets.*

Meanwhile, in VeVideer Forest, the noise Floral heard before was just a squirrel goofing around with its food. After ignoring it, she continues to walk through the weeds ahead cautiously.

Five minutes pass, and Floral hears another strange noise, and she starts following the rustling sound in the trees.

Suddenly, a small creature resembling a plant eases its head out of a bunch of leaves. It's staring at Floral, wondering who made the noise.

TRIITHE. *It lowers its head into the leaves quietly.*

Floral did not hear the little creature because of its quietness. She is concentrating on the other louder noise.

After two minutes of walking, she falls into a giant six-foot hole. The girl gets angry and summons her ability, chlorokinesis. She is carried out of the hole by a vine and steps off with her fists balled up.

Suddenly, someone threw a sword at her. Floral immediately raises a vine wall in front of her and instinctively lowers her head.

The sword slices through the vines and passes directly over her. A colossal knight comes out of hiding and starts charging at her, and he pushes her to a huge tree and pins her there.

Floral cannot move.

The knight backs away from the tree, forcibly grabs her, and throws her over his shoulder. He throws her with much intensity, and she smacks into another tree.

The knight walks over to his sword and picks it up. He is making his way to her. The girl is trying to use her chlorokinesis, but something is preventing her from doing so. She is suffering from bruises, and she is panicking.

The knight starts running while holding it close to his body. A portal opens under Floral, and she falls through. She lands in another part of the forest, far away from the big scary knight.

Meanwhile, back at the scene, the knight stops in his tracks, looking around the area, wondering where the girl escaped. A shadow boy bursts out of another portal and tries to impale the man from behind with a sharp metal pole, and it's broken once it contacts his armor. The knight turns his head. At the same time, he swings his sword, attempting to slice off this person's head. The boy teleports, just in time, avoiding the fatal strike. ShaVenger reappears in front of him, smiling.

SHAVENGER. Hey there! *He waves.*

He teleports again, reappearing in front of the knight. He punches the knight multiple times on his helmet, which is ineffective. His hands are now hurting but he continues his attacks and ignores the pain.

The boy launches his foot out before him and kicks off the knight's armor. The man grabs his right leg. ShaVenger becomes frightened and teleports into a goo-like substance. The knight lets go of his right leg just in time. The teen reappears in a tree, close to the knight's position, thinking about his next attack.

SHAVENGER. *He is rubbing his leg—* Big ass, baboon.

The knight hears a noise and throws his sword high into the tree in front of him like a boomerang. ShaVenger leans back and falls out of the tree, and he misses being hit by the sword's sharp blade.

The teen stands up, looking at him. The sword swings back around, going to the man, and he catches his sword. ShaVenger is observing the knight's next move.

Meanwhile, elsewhere in VeVideer Forest, Floral is sitting on the ground. She discovers her chlorokinesis also has a healing factor; however, she cannot heal fast enough.

The same little creature is crawling on branches and staring at her, quietly moving to different parts of the tree. It raises its head and stares at a small child wearing knight armor.

A small knight is watching Floral from a safe but very close distance. Floral gets surprised when she sees the miniature knight staring at her. He's also wearing a helmet to conceal his identity.

FLORAL. *She stands up slowly and carefully because her healing ability takes time.* Don't come any closer, or I'll vine your little butt!

The young child knight takes a step back and starts to run off in the other direction.

FLORAL. Thank you. *She falls on her behind, breathing slowly.*

A few minutes later, she hears a loud bang. The noise came from where the young knight ran. She limps to the area and sees a horde of statistabots surrounding the kid. He's holding his sword out in front of him. The bots start to attack with electricity.

Unfamiliar with fighting robotic creatures, the young knight blasts into a tree and drops his sword. His helmet falls off, revealing his true face.

Floral sees an innocent little boy. The young knight tries to grab his helmet before the bots attack again. They ready their electric attacks and are about to fire at him, and Floral uses her chlorokinesis to stop them. Vines emerge underneath the young boy's boots, taking each bot high into the air. She uses her V-Link to send the bots back to VICE HQ.

The girl stares at him. The boy grabs his helmet, places it back on his head, and then stands up.

Floral summons a vine to pick up his sword, and it hands the sword to him. The child looks at her cautiously. After scanning her for a few seconds, he grabs his weapon.

FLORAL. It's OK, and I'm not going to hurt you. *She stares at the boy for a while.* How did you become a—?

She senses danger. With quick thinking, she uses her ability to summon vines. They manage to turn the approaching sword; however, the hilt grazes her on the back of her head. She saved herself, just barely, from a severe head injury. The girl falls to the ground.

The big knight from before is slowly walking toward Floral and the young knight. The girl stands up slowly while holding the back of her head.

The unknown man is getting closer. Floral feels like crying. She falls to her knees, still holding the back of her head, quietly wishing her father was right by her side.

ShaVenger comes out of a portal, and roundhouse kicks the knight in the back of his head. He teleports away and reappears next to the young boy.

SHAVENGER. What the– I thought my statistabots captured your lil' butt by now? Pfft, I got to do *everything* around here! *He raises his arm, about to strike the young boy.*

FLORAL. *She raises her head, looking at the young knight.* No!!! *A vine picks her up, and she runs closer to the boy. She still feels unbearable pain coming from the back of her head. She sends a vine to slap his raised arm.* Leave him *alone*!! *She gets beside the young knight and stands next to him.*

SHAVENGER. *He shouts.* Look out!!!!

The scary knight charges at the cross-humans; Floral uses her chlorokinesis and puts up a wall of vines in front of them. He continues to charge straight and busts through it. ShaVenger pushes Floral out of the way. The knight grabs the teen and slams him into a tree.

The shadow boy groans. He turns completely black, and his body turns into a slimy liquid. The knight steps back.

This action surprises him. The girl watches her comrade, looking very concerned. The child knight watches the big scary knight, and Floral, very closely and takes two steps backward.

ShaVenger's slimy body moves ten regular footsteps away before his body turns solid again. The scary knight turns his head, watching.

The shadow teen's body is now whole again. The young child sprints to ShaVenger, raising his sword high. Once the young knight is close enough, he swings his sword, and ShaVenger dodges the attack and swings his left leg. The child flips over his left leg, landing next to the big knight. Someone shoots at the ground between the two cross-humans and the two knights.

SHAVENGER. *Before he looks up to figure out where the shot came from, he already knows.* Curse you, Z. *He raises his head and looks slightly to his right at the approaching agent.* Always interfering.

Floral's eyes follow Z, looking at him in the air, then she looks at the young knight. She is worried about him.

Agent Z descends from the sky, holding his blaster in one hand and holding a small object in the other hand. He is visually scanning the big scary knight.

SHAVENGER. *He looks at the two knights and points his finger at them.* We'll get you two some other time.

The shadow boy lowers his arm, and the two cross-humans teleport away individually.

Agent Z and the unknown man are looking at each other. Z lands on the ground, the exact spot where Floral was standing.

AGENT Z. So, there are knights in this world? *He is very shocked.* I feel you're grimacing at me under that ridiculously ugly helmet. *He laughs.*

The knight throws his left arm out, and the wind blasts in Z's direction. He raises his arms in front of his face. The mighty wind pushes him back, and he hits a tree. The wind stops, and the two knights are gone. The un-activated Invisi-Dome disappears in Z's hand.

AGENT Z. *He contacts VLORs HQ.* Agent Z to Commander Addams.

CO. ADDAMS. *He answers the call on his headset.* What is your report, Z?

AGENT Z. Well, it's true. These two knights in VeVideer Forest must've caused the small tremors. I mean, they are actual knights! There's a little one and a huge ugly one. They must've been training or something. I watched them for a while, and ShaVenger and Floral were down here trying to capture them both.

CO. ADDAMS. I see, and I'll be keeping you on this assignment. Discover why VICE wants these two knights and possibly find out about them.

AGENT Z. I will, sir.

CO. ADDAMS. That's what I like to hear. Stay safe. *He ends the call.*

AGENT Z. Now we've got knights. What else?

Meanwhile, Floral and ShaVenger arrive at the operations room at VICE HQ. The double doors slide open, and the two walk inside. Right next to the window is a man in a suit standing still and facing the wall. The suit is similar to Talgitx's. Floral stops walking, and ShaVenger continues to step closer.

SHAVENGER. *He mistakes the mystery man for a scientist.* Yo Mache, I *really* should be placed in charge. Z is interfering too damn much! Do you think you can put in a good word for m–

The mystery man turns around, facing the two cross-humans.

SHAVENGER. *He jumps back.* Whoa! You're not Mache!! *He turns his body black, ready to fight the intruder.*

FLORAL. *She stands there and is quiet.*

CO. XAVIER. Glad I get to see you cross-humans up close on my first day. *He walks past ShaVenger to the other side of the room and turns and faces the two cross-humans.* I want to see how complicated these VLORs agents can be.

SHAVENGER. *His body changes to solid black, and he's ready to fight this intruder.* Who are you?!

CO. XAVIER. *He stares at the teen for a minute before responding in a not-so-pleased tone.* Xavier. *He pauses for five seconds—* The true commander.

SHAVENGER. *He's in disbelief.* No way. Where's Talgitx?

FLORAL. *She whispers to herself.* No. Talgitx can't be gone. Can he?

CO. XAVIER. This is not your concern, cross-human.

SHAVENGER. *He frowns.* It's ShaVenger.

ShaVenger leaps off the floor, aiming at Xavier, but he doesn't move. When the boy is close to Xavier, the man backhands him across his face. He moved so fast you couldn't even see it coming. The teen falls on the hard, tiled floor, holding his throbbing face. The girl is at a loss for words.

CO. XAVIER. *He turns his head slightly, looking at her.* Do you want to be foolish like Joel Rodriguez here? Try something, Miss Eraine. Try the same stupid move. *He waits a while for any response from her.*

FLORAL. No sir. I'm good.

CO. XAVIER. *He looks at the boy in pain.* I know about that mouth, and that should remind you. *He pauses for a short while.* The mission you two just returned from, why did you return empty-handed?

ShaVenger stands up, carefully watching him. The force of Xavier's backhand smack did not appear to have been strong, but his vision went dark. He passed out, but he was still conscious. He slowly walks closer to Floral.

FLORAL. *She waited for her comrade to respond but decided to answer.* Agent Z interfered again, sir. He always does.

CO. XAVIER. Huh? *He is quiet for seven seconds.* I want to meet Agent Z and the other agents of VLORs for myself.

The two cross-humans retire to their quarters for the day.

Tuesday, June 20th, 2107

Floral is in her quarters, sitting on her bed, and places the picture of her father back on the nightstand beside her bed, and she thinks about the young knight she saw yesterday, remaining quiet the whole time.

FLORAL. The big knight *must* have him under a spell. I— I have to save him.

Meanwhile, Xavier travels to Canada on an assignment with twenty statistabots and ShaVenger.

They're at Mount Caubvick, a mountain near Labrador and Quebec, the Selamiut Range of the Torngat Mountains. In 2015, Mount Caubvick was one of the highest points in mainland Canada, east of Alberta.

The VICE commander is looking for someone; who can it be?

ShaVenger is halfway on the mountain and decides to sit on a huge boulder and place his left leg on a plant. Suddenly, the plant starts moving, and he becomes startled and stands, and the creature runs away.

SHAVENGER. *He yells.* Sir! I'm on it! *He commands the statistabots.* Go and get that plant thing! *He runs with them.*

Ten statistabots are closing in around the plant creature, and the other ten follow.

The shadow boy and the ten statistabots come to a halt. He curiously wonders what type of plant can move like that.

Xavier is far away from them but can see them clearly as day. He is walking to them at his own pace and closely watching them.

SHAVENGER. *He shouts to his statistabots.* All right, I want that thing in chains! Go and get it!!!!

All twenty statistabots fly at the plant creature, and it lowers itself to the ground. The statistabots shoot electricity, but their attacks are repelled back at them. Someone comes in fast; a strange female gets in between the creature and the bots.

This mystery girl pulls out a weapon and shields the creature.

ShaVenger orders the statistabots to shoot the mystery girl. She quickly leaps off the ground, landing on one bot at a time, and knocks out every last one. She lands before the plant creature and looks at the teen boy.

SHAVENGER. Oh. A challenge face, huh? All right, bet!

He teleports into a goo-like substance, reappears in front of her, and gets punched in the face. He falls on his back but quickly returns to his feet. He sends punches at her, and she moves her body in an unusual fighting style and avoids his attacks easily. The girl punches him in his chest, and the force of it knocks him off balance. The girl slides her left foot behind his right foot, and he falls on his butt.

The boy teleports, reappears in the same spot, and is surrounded by a condensed dust cloud that quickly subsides. The girl and the plant creature are gone.

Xavier stops walking and is now standing beside the boy. He is looking dead ahead with a smile on his face.

SHAVENGER. *He looks at his commander.* I'll get her next time. *He gulps.* I promise you, sir.

CO. XAVIER. *He's still looking dead ahead with a smile on his face.* Yes, you will.

Season 2, Episode 12

Wednesday, June 21, 2107

In the morning, at Gowdon's Prison, Dale Jr. is having breakfast in the cafeteria. He is sitting at a table full of savages. The prisoners he's seated with have no training in etiquette. He is not comfortable with these people, but he's no punk. These individuals tried to bully him when he first arrived, but he put them in their place.

The man finishes his breakfast and looks at the clock above the barred windows. He stands up, carries his tray to the garbage, places the empty tray on top of the garbage bin, and exits the cafeteria, returning to his cell. He passes by a guard, looks at him, grins, and continues walking to his cell.

Meanwhile, Team Kyros-X is plotting something on a warehouse's rooftop in Dowers City, Illinois. They are discussing how they will break Dale Jr. out of prison.

DOMOS. Mannnn. He's offering mad bank!

CLOUDIS MONROE. We break him out, and then we'll have to deal with ZEXTERN.

DOMOS. You scared? *He grins at Cloudis.*

RON BATTLETON. There's nothing to fear. ZEXTERN is gone for good.

CLOUDIS MONROE. When'd you hear this information?

RON BATTLETON. A bogus story has been playing on every local news station, and the U.S. Government sent S.W.A.T. to take them down. *He looks at the group and shakes his head. But we* all know who defeated ZEXTERN.

SNAKE. VLORs.

DOMOS. So, Dale Jr., What's he got to do with ZEXTERN?

CLOUDIS MONROE. He supplied them with SupeXoil, the stuff used to power my jet.

DOMOS. So, he snaked them? *He laughs.* Oh!! My dude!

SNAKE. I say we take the deal. With those resources– *He looks at Domos.* – Kyros X will be unbeatable!

DOMOS. Now you talkin' my lingo.

CLOUDIS MONROE. Let me get this straight. Do you wish to storm into a prison where VLORs have high security?

DOMOS. We got this, Cloud. You shouldn't worry much. Darkstras was never scared. *He pulls out a piece of paper from his pocket.* Someone contacted me from his business. Whoever this is, they would like Kyros-X to break him out.

CLOUDIS MONROE. *He's quiet for a while.* I have a plan.

DOMOS. Let's hear it.

They discuss a plan for a prison break. Meanwhile, Agent Rev is kicking around some statistabots near the beach, inside an Invisi-Dome, on New Waii Island.

AGENT REV. Oh Yeah! Let's R-R-Revvvvv up!

He charges in and battles the remaining bots, and uses his V-Link to activate his arm blaster, shooting every last one until their tiny pieces of metal.

AGENT REV. Oh! Oh! I killin' em! *He laughs child-like. His V-Link beeps, and he answers the call.* Hi, Commander.

CO. ADDAMS. Rev! I see you're handling the virtual training exercises perfectly well. I'm sorry we cannot bring you on board sooner. You're getting there!

AGENT REV. *He says with excitement in his voice.* Does mean I get to go to America and help the gold agent in his fight?!

CO. ADDAMS. Not quite. But I want to put you on an assignment with Agent Rahz. You'll be shadowing her.

AGENT REV. Okay, sir. I bet America awesome. I cannot wait to go!

CO. ADDAMS. I'll contact you soon. Oh! You will be getting an exceptional vehicle to travel over rough terrain. *He pauses on the headset.* Okay. Your V-Link has received a gift. Look in your inventory. You'll love it! Over and out. *He hangs up the call.*

AGENT REV. *He looks through his inventory to discover a vehicle. He materializes the new cycle.* Ayyyeee!!! *He giggles.* Yesh, yesh, Yesh!! I'm going to rev up now!

Meanwhile, Xavier is in his office, sitting in Talgitx's old chair. He is sitting alone in the dark, soft-lit office, watching a recording of the local news that happened on June 11th. A lady is on the big screen. She's in a blue dress, has long brunette hair, and looks to be in her mid-forties. She is talking about a crime in Hidendale Springs.

UNNAMED NEWSCASTER FEMALE. ...Crime in Hidendale Springs! How a speeding semi-truck struck two locals? One killed, and one tragically wounded. When we return after this commercial break, we'll dive more into it.

The man stands up, walks to the door, and exits his office. That afternoon, Domos, Ron, and Snake are inside a maintenance van driving to Gowdon's Prison front gates.

SNAKE. We need ID's.

DOMOS. Cloudis took care of it.

The van pulls up to the front gates. A guard walks up, asking for vehicle registration and license information, and Ron hands it to him.

UNNAMED SECURITY GUARD. I didn't know maintenance was today. *He scans their documents.*

DOMOS. *He is sitting in the back of the van.* Damn! You guys act like we're about to bust someone out of here!

SNAKE. Shhh! *He looks at the security guard.* Don't mind my psycho friend here, officer. This guy knows what it's like to be —*He whispers*— an inmate's chubi.

DOMOS. *He shakes his head.* Uh-huh. Keep talkin' shit, you ophidian heist man.

UNNAMED SECURITY GUARD. *He hands back all paperwork.* Alright, you guys are good to go. *He turns his head and speaks to the other guard.* They're good. Open the gate and let them through.

DOMOS. *He grins.* Alright, let's get it!

Meanwhile, Zhariah sits at the top of Drenden Mountain, the side away from the Observatory. She has been here for over an hour.

ZHARIAH. *She sighs and stares at the sky.* It's peaceful up here. *She's thinking about this past month, focusing on Michel's death.*

Tears begin to fall down her face.

Meanwhile, Xavier is parked at Crumarus Hospital. He gets inside his shiny SUV and drives away.

After twenty minutes of driving, Xavier reaches Tarainound Street. Xavier drives his vehicle and parks in a designated parking spot near a sidewalk.

Five minutes later, he walks out of a convenience store, finishing a breakfast burrito. He walks to his vehicle when he gets a strange feeling.

Meanwhile, Zhariah is making her way down the mountain. There are wooden stairs near tall trees and thick bushes. Unknowingly, she passes DiLusion, and he is hiding behind a tall tree.

The girl wipes her tears with her right sleeve as she goes down the mountain.

After ten minutes, she makes it to the bottom safely. She walks down the street, heading home. DiLusion comes out of hiding with an unusual grin on his face.

After a couple of minutes, DiLusion follows the girl down a pathway to the city. There's a reasonable distance between them. Xavier eerily walks out from between two trees on the man's right with a smirk, stopping him from pursuing the girl.

The VICE commander has his hands in his pockets.

CO. XAVIER. *He stops walking and smiles. He turns his body, facing DiLusion.* What's this—? *He stops smiling.* —abducting children?

DILUSION. *He chuckles.* Wild thoughts you have. *He shakes his head and he starts walking.*

Once he reaches Xavier, the man places his right arm out, stopping DiLusion from going anywhere. He stops and looks at Xavier.

CO. XAVIER. *He lowers his arm.* What's your hurry?

DILUSION. *He is getting a strange feeling.* You are in my way.

CO. XAVIER. *Scoffs.* Like you have anywhere to go. So listen up. I have been looking for someone with your unique abilities. Have you heard about VLORs?

DILUSION. *He is disconcerted.* Heh. Do you need my help?

CO. XAVIER. I'm not one to lie. But yes, I do.

DILUSION. *He is smiling.* Well, how can I help you?

CO. XAVIER. Just remember my request. I'll come looking for you when I am ready.

Xavier walks down the path. When he is far enough, DiLusion turns his head and whispers.

DILUSION. What a terrifying feeling I get from him. *He pauses for five seconds, then turns around and disappears into a portal.*

Xavier was watching him discreetly after he teleported away.

CO. XAVIER. *He walks to his vehicle.* Very unique indeed!

Meanwhile, the maintenance van pulls up to the Primous Facility, and the three men exit the vehicle and make their way into the building.

DOMOS. You're a go, Snake. *He looks at Ron.* You incapacitate the guards. I'll be behind you.

Snake stands by the vent outside of the building. He touches the building and camouflages himself to it. He takes off the vents cover and crawls inside. Ron walks to the security room, still wearing the maintenance uniform, and Domos walks behind him.

Meanwhile, Dale Jr. is inside his cell reading a romance novel, and he remembers his old flame back in high school.

In his reptilian form, Snake crawls through the vents and locates the man's cell. He looks down into the room.

DALE JR. *He hears a faint noise, sounding like a snake's hiss.* What was that?

The facility has gone quiet for some reason.

Domos is walking behind Ron, knocking out all guards quickly. Ron walks into the control room, finds the locking switch to Dale's cell, and disarms it. Domos is happily making his way upstairs.

DOMOS. Money, Money! *He peeks into Dale's cell.* Yoo-hoo, Boss! Are ya in there?

DALE JR. I am. Could you be any louder? *He stands up.*

Snake busts out of the ceiling's vent and stands in front of the man. Dale unpleasantly looks at him.

DALE JR. Seriously, you're looking rather—

SNAKE. *He steps closer to Dale.* Don't anger me, Mr. Falakar! *He hisses.* Remember, I'm here to save you!

DALE JR. I wasn't *even* going—

DOMOS. *He walks up to them, smiling. He places his arms around their shoulders.* Boys, boys! Let's act like men, shall we? *He removes his arms.*

RON BATTLETON. *He shouts to the second level.* Hey! What are you doing up there?! Get him, and let's go already!

DOMOS. *He shouts to Ron.* Roger that!! *He turns around and faces Snake and Dale.* I swear, it's like *he's* the boss!

DALE JR. The man is right. *He straightens his shirt collar and walks out of his cell.*

DOMOS. *He follows Dale, and he jokes.* So, shall we take you to your "private island" to recuperate? *He laughs.*

DALE JR. Pfft, like I have one at the moment. No! We visit the board of directors at Stratum Oil Industries.

SNAKE. *He transforms back to human form.* Which location?

DALE JR. *He turns his head and looks at him while smiling—all of them.* First, we'll go to the one in College Station, Texas.

DOMOS. Alright, we're off!

The three KYRO-X members walk to the staircase leading downstairs. A security guard, lying next to Ron Battleton, wakes up. He reaches for a button near Ron's leg and presses it. An alarm sounds throughout the entire place, and Ron turns and kicks him across his face. The guard is out cold again.

RON BATTLETON. Shit! I'm getting sloppy. *He reaches inside his pocket, pulls out a small detonator, and tapes it to the security guy's forehead.* I'd like to see you roll over now.

As Ron knocked out all the guards in prison and made his way to Dale's cell, Domos was placing bombs around the facility.

DOMOS. *He meets Ron outside the control room.* Where's the detonator?

SNAKE. *He is shocked.* The what?!

DOMOS. Chill.

RON BATTLETON. We have no time. I failed to incapacitate a guard, and he pressed a silent alarm. I say we have— a little over a minute before someone arrives or until one of them rolls on their forehead.

SNAKE. What does that mean?

RON BATTLETON. Don't worry about it.

DOMOS. *He tightens his fists.* Ooooooohh, I swear! What was Cloudis thi—

RON BATTLETON. *He raises his guns, pointing them at Domos.* Go ahead. Finish your sentence.

DALE JR. *He slowly places his hands on the guns, lowering them.* Relax. *He looks at Domos.* Where's your getaway vehicle?

DOMOS. Follow me.

Domos leads the way, running to the facility's exit and going outside the doors.

Z and Rahz teleport inside the prison; the two agents notice all the guards are unconscious. Z finds one guard with a detonator taped on his forehead and disarms it. The two immediately search the grounds.

KYROS-X and Dale Jr are inside the maintenance van, making their way to Cloudis's jet, parked on top of a parking garage. Z is riding his flight board, and Rahz utilizes her hover boots, skating two inches off the ground.

They see a black jet and it's taking off. They materialize their blasters and open fire. The jet ignites its turbo engine, and it zooms out of sight. Z lands on the ground, and Rahz lands beside him.

AGENT Z. *He snaps his fingers.* Shoot!! How did that jet get away so quickly?! *His eyes fixated on the sky.*

AGENT RAHZ. SupeXoil. It helps machines— anything with an engine— go faster!

AGENT Z. *He looks at his comrade.* I bet it was Pogo again.

AGENT RAHZ. *She looks at him, raises her right arm, and checks her V-Link.* Something tells me it was—. *She calls VLORs.* Agent Rahz to Commander Addams, do you copy?

AGENT Z. It was who?! You didn't finish! *He shakes his head, watching the surroundings as she finishes her call with the commander.*

AGENT RAHZ. *She finishes her conversation with Addams and hangs up.* Are you ready to go?

AGENT Z. Yes. *He teleports.*

Rahz smiles then she teleports. Meanwhile, Xavier is standing at the Qwinzale's Convenience Store checkout counter, purchasing a few snacks.

The man looks around and focuses on two women, one in her late forties and another in her mid-thirties. The older woman grabs her grocery bags and starts walking to the exit, and the other woman follows behind her. He overhears a little of their conversation.

ANBIGALA REEDS. We must carefully discuss how my organization can better assist those children's futures. You cannot continue to do this by yourself.

ABIGAIL JOHNSON. *She is exiting the store.* I have been doing just fine for twenty-two years.

ANBIGALA REEDS. *She exits the store and walks to her right.* The funding you told me you're getting is insufficient to care for ten children properly. *She sighs.* Listen closely.

ABIGAIL JOHNSON. *She stops walking and turns her body to face her.* I have been hearing your lectures for almost a year! I do not wish to have your funding, Ms. Reeds! Please bother another.

Two little boys run up to Auntie momma, stopping right before her.

CAIL and ADAM. *They speak at the same time.* Do you need help with the groceries? *They both extend their arms.*

ABIGAIL JOHNSON. *She keeps her eyes on Anbigala. She hands the groceries to Cail and Adam.* Store these in the proper places.

CAIL and ADAM. *They grab the groceries and run to the building.* We will!

ANBIGALA REEDS. *Her attitude changes a little.* I have not come here to pick a fight with you, Mrs. Johnson.

ABIGAIL JOHNSON. Then please excuse yourself, Ms. Reeds. I am fine! My children are fine!

ANBIGALA REEDS. *She reaches into her handbag.* I did not wish to have to do this, but– *She pulled out a few forms.* If you do not act soon, these children will be taken away and placed in better homes.

ABIGAIL JOHNSON. *Her expression changes and she appears to have had her heart ripped in half. She takes the papers out of her hands and reads them.*

ANBIGALA REEDS. I see I have your attention now. *She sighs.* I'm sorry, Mrs. Johnson. I know you love these children dearly, but they deserve better.

ABIGAIL JOHNSON. *She almost tears up.* You–

A young man approaches the two women before Abigail can speak.

XAVIER. *He approaches.* Pardon me. *He extends his hand to the social worker.* My name is Xavier.

ANBIGALA REEDS. *She shakes his hand—a* pleasure to meet you.

XAVIER. *He shakes and extends his hand to the other woman.* Pleasure meeting you as well. *He smiles.*

ABIGAIL JOHNSON. *She hesitates for a few seconds and then shakes his hand—a* pleasure.

ANBIGALA REEDS. *She looks back at Abigail.* I shall leave those with you, and you can ring me on my phone when you decide. *She walks to her car, a shiny and black car resembling an SUV, parked on the curb near the foster care.* Good day to you too, Xavier!

Anbigala starts her car and drives off.

ABIGAIL JOHNSON. *She tears up at the thought of losing her children. She sniffs.* I'm sorry. *She uses her left sleeve to wipe her tears.*

XAVIER. No! *He takes out his handkerchief.* Use mine. *He hands it to her.*

ABIGAIL JOHNSON. *She politely takes it and wipes her tears away.* Thank you.

XAVIER. No problem. *He smiles.* Let me walk with you.

Xavier walks her home.

XAVIER. I am sorry, but I was eavesdropping back in the convenience mart. Does she want to separate you from your children?

ABIGAIL JOHNSON. It would be best if you weren't eavesdropping but yes. You heard right.

XAVIER. I can help you fight back! If– you'll allow my assistance.

ABIGAIL JOHNSON. I need some time.

XAVIER. You take all the time you need.

The two approach the foster home, and Abigail thanks him for being so lovely and walks inside the building.

XAVIER. *He takes one last look before turning around and walking down the sidewalk.*

Thursday, June 22, 2107

The next day, at Stratum Oil Industries, in College Station, Texas, the board of directors is having a business meeting. They are discussing how to re-brand Stratum Oil Industries. A guard, who is doing his rounds, interrupts their discussion.

UNNAMED SECURITY GUARD. My apologies. I have a gentleman here, and he would like a moment of your time.

MOWTON JOHNSON. What are you doing? Close the damn door!

JOAN MLINTON. Where are your manners, Mr. Johnson? *She turns her attention to the guard.* Sure. We have a few minutes to hear what he has to say! *She smiles.*

ARU JUSINOWO. Yes. Bring him in.

CRISTALE NEWJUNE. Tell him to make it quick.

Clinton Bauher sits there and doesn't say a word.

Mowton Johnson is a middle-aged African American male. He has a nice complexion and wavy hair and likes wearing stylish suits.

Cristale Newjune is a middle-aged woman in her late forties. She is Caucasian American. She is rude, but only if you interrupt something important she has going on. She wears skirts, fingertip length. Her hair is up in a bun, and she wears tiny glasses. The glasses are down on her nose. She's wearing heels on her feet.

Aru Jusinowo originates from Saudi Arabia. He is in his mid-forties. He wears an all-white suit with a crimson tie. His hair's slicked back. You can tell he used a lot of hair grease. His face has a few blemishes, but you can barely see them.

Joan Mlinton is a young Filipina-Caucasian American female. She carries herself divinely. She wears white leggings with a long top, resembling a dress. The top is slightly too high, but you can't see anything inappropriate with the leggings. She wears red high heels, and her complexion appears to be flawless.

Clinton Bauher is your typical average Caucasian American. He is purebred, which may seem hard to believe. He is the oldest one in the room. He is an old guy, around the age of fifty to sixty. He has on a black suit with a black tie. He wears glasses and missing hair on top of his head.

The roaming guard closes the door. Seconds later, a man opens the door and steps inside the room. He closes the door and turns to face the board of directors. The look on their faces is like they just stepped on something nasty when you walk down an alley in a dirty neighborhood. All of them except Miss Mlinton.

CLINTON BAUHER. *The look on his face is priceless.* Dale? *He stands up.*

DALE JR. Don't bother standing. *He walks to the front of the room.*

MOWTON JOHNSON. *He is now calm.* Who even let you in the building, Dale?

DALE JR. *He smirks.* Yes! Who *wouldn't* let me into *my* building?!

ARU JUSINOWO. *He stutters with fear in his voice.* D—Dale. We were ju—

DALE JR. *He throws his hand up at him.* Save it. *He looks at Mlinton. He points.* I don't know you. Care to tell me who you are, Belle femme!

JOAN MLINTON. *She blushes and then laughs.* Don't flirt with me, Dale! You wouldn't know how to handle this—

MOWTON JOHNSON. *He rises from his seat in anger.* Alright, that's enough! Would you kindly *exit* the premises before the authorities arrest you for trespassing?

DALE JR. *He's laughing uncontrollably.* Mowton. *He is still laughing his butt off*—the same guy as when my father owned this company.

MOWTON JOHNSON. *He pulls out his cell phone.* I'm calling the police.

Dale Jr. pulls out a loaded .9 mm pistol, puts it on the conference room table, and places his hands in his pockets. Mowton Johnson turns off his phone and sets it back in his jacket.

MOWTON JOHNSON. You wouldn't dare.

DALE JR. Oh! I wouldn't. *He paces back and forth. You all* voted me out of *my* father's company. The one I inherited! Oh, I would. Especially you.

MOWTON JOHNSON. Just do it, then. Why are you hesitating?

DALE JR. Hmmmm. I don't know.

Someone knocks on the door to the conference room and opens the door. Team Kyros-X walks inside, and they are unarmed. Well, they are still trying to figure out Ron Battleton.

DOMOS. *He walks closer to Dale Jr. while pretending to admire the decor around the office.* Lovely! Mhm. *He snickers and looks at the board of directors.* Damn! Yo, Cloudis bro. *He points at Joan Mlinton.* Can I take her home? *He grins and licks his lips.*

JOAN MLINTON. *She looks at him in disgust.* Eww.

CLOUDIS MONROE. *He slaps Domos's hand back down and steps in front of him, looking at the board of directors. He speaks to Dale.* The explosives are in place.

ARU JUSINOWO. *He is terrified.* You're going to blow us up?!

MOWTON JOHNSON. *He sighs.* Of course, he is, Aru. *He places his hands in his pockets.* Mr. Falakar had to hire a few thugs to do his dirty work. How pretentious of you.

DOMOS. Yo, if you don't— *He shouts.* Shut it!! I'm going to knock yo' punk ass out!

MOWTON JOHNSON. Do you see what I mean? *He looks at the other board of directors.* This lunatic is upset about losing his company and wants to kill the people making his company *earn money*!! *He stares at Dale.*

Ron Battleton grabs Mr. Johnson from behind and places him in an inescapable position.

DOMOS. *He raises his voice, getting all excited.* Thank... you... Ron!!

MOWTON JOHNSON. *He is struggling but cannot get out of his grip.* You...

SNAKE. *He's standing near the door and leaning on the wall.* He still got something to say. *He shakes his head.*

All the other board of directors stands up. They are watching Mowton, and then they glance up at Dale.

DALE JR. So, it had to come to this. Don't be alarmed! You guys wanted to play. *He starts grinning.* So, let's play!

CLOUDIS MONROE. I would hurry this along, Dale. The chargers will go off in thirty minutes.

DOMOS. Mooooooooore than enough time! You worry too much.

DALE JR. Cloudis. *He leans in closer and speaks low, and the others can hear him.* You guys did a fantastic job. Thank you! Now take the others to the lobby. *He looks at the five board members.* I want *no one* to exit the premises.

CLOUDIS MONROE. You got it. *He nods at the other members of Kyros-X.*

All of Team Kyros-X exit the room, and Domos walks out last. Before he's entirely out of the room, he blows a kiss at Joan. The woman turns away, looks at the floor, and her face turns red.

MOWTON JOHNSON. You're going to *jail* for this!

DALE JR. Ha! Not after the new headline comes out tomorrow. *He looks at Mowton and winks his left eyelid at him.*

MOWTON JOHNSON. What're you talking about?

DALE JR. Before coming here, I spoke to a friend. He works for the local newspaper. *He grins.*

CLINTON BAUHER. Dale, my friend. Please don't do this.

ARU JUSINOWO. Yes, please! I have a wife and kids. There are below the ages of ten and seven years old! Think about them, please!

JOAN MLINTON. Yes! Could you think of the children and me too? *She starts to fake cry.* I'm too damn young to die!

CRISTALE NEWJUNE. *She rolls her eyes.* Oh, lord. You know what, Dale? All my babies are grown, and I can give two shits if you kill us.

JOAN MLINTON. Yeah, you wouldn't.

CLINTON BAUHER. *He is getting annoyed.* Oh my god, would you all— *He shouts.* Shut–up! *He walks closer to Dale.* Let's talk about this. You can have 40% of the company back.

MOWTON JOHNSON. *He shouts.* Don't give him shit!

JOAN MLINTON. Dale, please, I had nothing to do with you being voted—

DALE JR. *He raises his hand, and they all become silent.* Look at what you guys have become. *He points at Mowton.* Well, except for him.

MOWTON JOHNSON. Yeah, screw you, too, buddy! You psycho.

Dale Jr. laughs and walks out of the room.

MOWTON JOHNSON. No, screw this! *He speed walks behind Dale and tries to leave the room.*

Dale stops walking and gets in front of him. He looks at Dale and throws a punch. Dale leans back, avoiding it, and punches Mowton in his face. The man places his hands on his nose to keep the blood from gushing. The two women gasp.

DALE JR. Is there anyone else? *He looks at Aru and Clinton.* Do you two want to try something?

They both remain quiet, and Dale exits the room, shutting the door. The board members are terrified. A few minutes later, the entrance to the conference room explodes, and the actual door shoots across the room. Someone throws Dale inside, and he hits the back wall.

A girl steps inside, eyes angrily sweeping around the room, looking for Dale. She de-materializes her blaster. Within seconds, the board of directors hit the floor and fell unconscious. A boy much younger than the girl enters the room.

????? ???. *He looks at the board of directors. He speaks Portuguese.* Uau! (Whoa!)

????? ????. *She looks at him for a second, then looks back at Dale, lying on the floor.* English, Rev.

AGENT REV. Hehehee! *He smiles while closing his eyes.* Sorry, Rahz. *He stops smiling, looks at the board of directors, and then at Dale.* They drop. Why is he not under effects of Invisi-Dome powers?

AGENT RAHZ. Good question.

DALE JR. *He stands up and rubs his head.* Not– another one. *He smiles at Rahz.* But it is a *pleasure* to meet you again, young lady.

She speeds to him and punches him in his stomach, and he grabs his midsection and falls on the floor.

AGENT REV. *He looks away.* Ohhhh!!!! *He looks at the man.* That ha-urt (hurt)?

DALE JR. *He moans.* Yes, it did.

AGENT RAHZ. *She shouts.* Shut it! *She lowers her voice.* You don't deserve to talk.

DALE JR. *He is suffering from her punch, holding his stomach.* Are you sure you have *time* to waste here, watching over me right now? *He spits blood on the floor.* Stratum Oil is going to go up in smoke! *He starts laughing.*

AGENT RAHZ. *She points behind her at Rev.* He disarmed your explosives.

AGENT REV. —*and* buddies on team! *He smiles.* I did all by myself!

DALE JR. *He is still laughing, but then he stops.* You kids are so dumb. *He looks at the agents.* How many Stratum Oils are there? *He starts smiling again.*

AGENT RAHZ. *Her eyes go wide.* No.

AGENT REV. *He was looking at the girl.* What goin' on, Rahz?

DALE JR. Yes, my little foreign agent. Your friend just realized that I rigged another one of my buildings with explosives because I knew *you* would show.

AGENT RAHZ. *She quickly turns her head and looks at her comrade.* Rev, get your bike and meet me downstairs!

AGENT REV. *He nods.* Aye! *He runs out of the room, heading downstairs.*

DALE JR. You can try to make it there in ti— *He is punched in the face.*

AGENT RAHZ. *She slaps V-Cuffs on him, and you* better wish there's no explosion. *She drags him to the window.*

The girl opens the window, raises her right arm, and checks her V-Link for the closest Stratum Oil. The digital three-dimensional map shows that the next Stratum Oil is in Port Aransas, Texas, near Nueces County, Texas, approximately four hours from College Station, Texas, by car.

The girl activates the hovering ability in her boots, grabs Dale, and speeds out the window. Rev races toward her on his motorcycle. Together, they rush to Port Aransas to try to stop the Stratum Oil from exploding. As they departed from the Stratum Oil facility in College Station, the Invisi-Dome disappeared. The board members all wake up, wondering how they got on the floor.

Meanwhile, a young teen girl walks through the old Detroit-Windsor Tunnel, the fourth international border crossing between Michigan and Canada. It's an underground tunnel connecting Interstate 75 in Detroit with Highway 401 in Windsor, and the tunnel opened in 1930. In 2107, no vehicle has permission to cross this old international underwater crossing. The tunnel collapsed in the year 2040, creating a gorge. The first year, the tunnel flooded with water, but after the years, the water dried up in a few places. The girl is walking with a small plant creature.

The teen girl is walking fast-paced, and the tiny creature has trouble keeping up.

It shows that it is dehydrated. The girl is trying to get to a safe zone quickly to avoid another attack by electricity robots.

The creature collapses. The girl stopped walking after she heard something hit the ground. She turns her head, sees the animal has passed out due to dehydration and runs to its side. She reaches into her supply kit inside her utility belt for the last bit of water and pours it over its head, drenching it in a shower. The creature wakes, feeling alive and showing that it's full of energy.

???. *She is upset.* Oh, Kysis. *She has a foreign accent and some Asian dialect.* Now, what're we going to do about water?

Kysis makes a purring sound and rubs its body against the girl's right leg. Lin gently scratches the top of her head.

LIN. It's not your fault. *She looks around.* We have to keep moving. The darkness will creep on us faster than a hawk, and let's not give the darkness boy and his minions a chance to catch up to us.

They continue walking south. They are walking on a rocky path leading them to the state of Michigan.

Meanwhile, Agents Rahz and Rev arrive at Port Aransas, making their way to the Stratum Oil. It's close, and Rev accelerates on his bike, which can stay airborne.

AGENT RAHZ. *She yells.* Slow down!!

The boy speeds faster, getting closer to the building. After twenty seconds, All three arrive at Stratum Oil. The agents are hovering over the building when it suddenly blows up. The force of the explosion knocks Rev off his bike, and he flies backward and smacks into another nearby building. The girl drops Dale's un-immobilized body into the flames, and she, too, is blasted away. The fire is spreading fast. Rahz stands up, and so does Rev. He is coughing as he stares at the flames.

AGENT REV. R— R— Rahz. Is he d— d—? *He is terrified.*

AGENT RAHZ. *She gulps.* Let's get Dale Jr. quickly! Activate your V-Haler.

AGENT REV. How? *He looks at her.*

The girl uses her V-Link, and her V-Haler materializes—a protective body suit equipped to protect agents from terrible flames.

The boy copies her, and two agents run inside the burning building. Rahz throws out an Invisi-Dome and covers the entire area. The young agents stay together and fight the fires, trying their hardest to find Dale Jr.

The flames are becoming too much for even their V-Halers. After ten minutes, their air supply starts to run low. Rahz signals Rev, and the two jump out of a broken and melted window. They fall to the ground, stand up and run away from the burning building, reaching a safe distance.

AGENT REV. *He is panicking. He starts shouting.* Whadda we do, whadda we do?!

AGENT RAHZ. *She lowers her head, looking at the pavement, trying to stop herself from letting tears fall.* I—I'm sorry. *She sniffs.*

AGENT REV. *He turns his head and looks at her, and he is worried.* Rahz?

AGENT RAHZ. *She shakes her head repeatedly while eyeing the burning building.* I didn't mean to drop him. *She screams.* And why isn't the Invisi-Dome restoring the building?!

The girl calms herself. She breathes in and out three times and comes up with an idea. She activates her V-Link, materializes a V-Inducer, and throws it as far as she can at the burning building. The device enlarges and encloses itself around the burning building. There is a tiny burst of sound that goes off inside. The V-Inducer returns to standard size and de-materializes. The Stratum Oil building is undamaged, and there are no burn marks or signs of a fire. The device and the Invisi-Dome helped to restore the building to its previous state. Unfortunately, the building is not a Stratum Oil anymore. Agent Rev is amazed.

AGENT RAHZ. *She stares.* It wasn't supposed to change anything.

AGENT REV. What you mean?

AGENT RAHZ. The V-Inducer was supposed to take the fire off the building and burn bricks and other damages. This one might be defective. *She remembers Dale Jr.*

The two agents switch to stealth mode and look around the area for Dale Jr.'s charred corpse. After searching for five minutes, they found nothing. Rahz decides they should leave, and Rev hears strange sounds nearby, and he runs off, and the girl follows.

The boy runs behind the old Stratum Oil into an alley. He discovers a person lying on the ground. Dale Jr. is hiding under a dumpster, holding the right side of his face with his right hand. Rahz helps Rev pull him out. To their surprise, the fire burned the right side of his face to its unrecognizable point. They take him to the closest hospital; he's rushed into surgery upon arrival.

AGENT REV. Rahz.

AGENT RAHZ. Yes?

AGENT REV. Always this bad?

AGENT RAHZ. *She gulps.* No, Rev, It isn't.

Meanwhile, Team Kyros-X is arrested and sent to Gowdon's Prison. Doctors at Saint Caper Medical Facility cared for Dale Jr's wounds. Due to an assassination attempt on the board of directors at Stratum Oil, he is taken to Primous Facility by Agent Caj.

A VLORs operative, Angela Runn, sent a gift. Despite what he had done, she felt sorry about what happened to him and sent him a metallic mask to cover the right side of his face.

Friday, June 23, 2107

The next day, Lin and Kysis are walking along the side of an abandoned road. There are no signs to tell where they are, unfortunately. They continue walking forward, even after stopping at a four-way intersection. Kysis climbs on Lin's shoulders to rest.

A clean and shiny vehicle is driving down the opposite road. Lin is now half a mile from the four-way intersection. The car stops at the corner, and a young man, wearing an all-white suit, gets out of the passenger side. He stares in the direction the girl is walking.

?????. *He is in the driver's seat.* What's the matter with you?

?????. Nothing, Gobon. *He gets back inside the vehicle.* Let's hurry to Valousse City and get to work.

GOBON. Right, Navas. *He puts the vehicle in drive and continues straight.* Oooooohhh! That Air Clan Knight is gon' *to wish* he never returned!

NAVAS. It's been too long, and our ascendants waited until the day he would awaken from his slumber. They have prepared us for this moment. We're lucky to be the ones to open a can of whoop ass on Mageario.

GOBON. Hell Yeah! Mageario better watch his back! He messed with both of our clans. That isn't gon' fly by the two of us. He's going dooooown!! *He starts speeding down the road.*

Monday, June 26, 2107

The summer semester has two more weeks remaining. Zhariah and Katie hung out every day at summer school and outside of school. Katie even played at local parks with Zhariah's siblings, and Zhariah visited her family once. However, Katire had yet to see Zhariah's home.

This Monday morning at Centransdale High School, Zhariah finds her friend kneeling by the side of the school, and she is in tears.

ZHARIAH. *She walks closer to her friend, kneels, and places her arms around her shoulders.* What's wrong?

KATIRE. *She's crying. Tears are falling down her face.* I— try. *Sniffs.* E—Everything I d—

ZHARIAH. *She hurts to see that her friend is sad. She rubs the girl's back then she assumes something.* Was it Delena and Marie?

KATIRE. *She explodes, raising her voice.* Why does everyone always pick on me?! Delena— She keeps pushing me on the ground and calling me names!! *She has her face pressed against Zari's chest, crying.* It's not fair!

ZHARIAH. *She is holding her friend close. She doesn't know how to help.* I— I'm sorry, K— Katie. *She starts tearing up.*

KATIRE. *She has her arms around the girl's midsection, hugging her tight. Her head is resting on her chest.*

The two friends hug for five minutes. Katie sniffs and pulls away.

ZHARIAH. Are you feeling a little better?

KATIRE. *She is wiping the tears from her eyes.* A little bit. *Sniffs.* It's okay. Last night, I took some pills to help ease the pain.

ZHARIAH. *She becomes worried.* What— *She pauses.* —kind of pills?

KATIRE. *Sniffs.* I don't know. They were in my mom's closet, and many were inside an orange see-through container. *She sniffs again and pauses, looking at the grass under her and then at Zhariah.* I— I can't do— anymo—. *She sobs and weeps, placing her hands on her face.*

The girl places her left hand on Katire's right shoulder. After ten seconds, Zari notices the girl is fidgeting oddly. Katire's body starts to shake, and it's like her body is vibrating. Katire's breathing starts to slow down. Zari is watching her friend, trying to catch her breath.

Five seconds later, the girl collapsed on the grass, falling on her chest. Zari closes her eyes tight, trying hard not to cry. She quickly places her right hand under Katire's body to feel for a heartbeat, and it is faint. Zari screams out, and tears fall.

ZHARIAH. *She is holding onto Katire and shouting.* Help!! *Tears fill her eyes.* Please, someone! Help!!!! *She's crying over the girl's body.*

Professor Zow hears someone shouting from the school's parking lot and runs toward the noise. He sees Zari on the ground, crying over Katire's body, and he dials the emergency number on his phone.

Luckily, an ambulance was driving past and received the dispatcher's call.

Thursday, June 29, 2107

A few days passed, and after hearing nothing from Katire's parents or her teachers, Zari believed Katire had died.

All her life, Katie struggled to make friends. She tried everything, especially being herself, but no one wanted to befriend her. Zhariah is an exception, but unfortunately, Katire was suffering too much on the inside.

Before she met Zari, she always sat alone at lunch hour all the time at her old school and was always alone in the hallways, by her locker, and between classes.

Meanwhile, a few hours prior, Max Gerald and Pogo got on the GoRail Alpha Line train somewhere in Indiana. The train is now arriving at Laroouse City, Illinois.

They exit the train. Max walks to the stairs, and Pogo walks to the escalator and elevator, blocking the exits. The people trying to leave the subway station stare at them. Two men try to force their way through, and Max deals with them with brute force. For a skinny guy, he can deliver a punch. Pogo rips off his disguise, revealing his skin-tight suit with special devices on his ankles, enabling him to bounce around, and Max pulls out a .9 mm.

MAX GERALD. *He is grinning, clearly enjoying himself.* People, people. *He thinks and plays with his chin with his free hand.* Let's see. *He points.* Hey, Mogo. That spot looks *perfect* for letting the gas out. Don't you agree?

POGO. *He has an unidentifiable accent.* I told you my name's Pogo. *He scoffs.* Yeah, that is a good location. *He whispers silently to himself*—you lanky giraffe.

MAX GERALD. Oh boy! *He shoots his .9 mm at the ceiling.* Oh, noooo!! *He looks at a terrified, innocent child.* Luckily that wasn't you. *He laughs maniacally.*

Suddenly, something zooms down the stairs and passes the crazy criminal. The subway station is free of civilians.

POGO. *He is speaking in his unidentifiable accent, and he looks disappointed.* Oh, great.

MAX GERALD. *He is overly excited.* Oh boy! They're here; they're here!! *He is chuckling.*

Agents Z and Rev appear. They are standing between the stairs and the escalator. Rev's facing Max, and Z is facing Pogo.

AGENT REV. Hay! *He points at Max Gerald.* Es that crazy psycho guy? *He puts his hand down.*

AGENT Z. Yup. *He sighs.* You know what? Let's switch opponents.

AGENT REV. Fine wiff me.

The two agents switch positions.

POGO. *Speaking in his unidentifiable accent.* Switching makes *no* difference!! *He spits on the ground.*

AGENT REV. *He looks at the spit on the ground and then at Pogo.* Ugh! Nasssty!

AGENT Z. *He is shaking his head.* Yup! He's a spitter. *He turns his attention to Max Gerald.* So, what were you going to do this time?

MAX GERALD. Why don't you stay and find out? *He charges at a seemingly distracted agent.* Watch out in front of you! Heheh! *He swings a rusted metal pole at Z.*

AGENT Z. *He leans back, grabs the rusted pole, and kicks him in his abdomen. He lets go of the bar.*

Pogo hops toward Rev, who has his head turned, looking at Z, and slaps him on his head.

AGENT REV. *He grabs his head with both hands.* Heyy!! *He growls and charges at him.*

Pogo is hopping away, and Rev is trying to land an attack, but he keeps jumping away. The boy grins and materializes a Vactra Bopper on his right hand.

AGENT REV. *He chuckles.* I'm fast too! I *rev* up! *The flight devices in his boots activate. He lifts off the ground and starts skating two inches off the ground and on the walls. He is moving incredibly fast but can control where he is going. He zooms past Pogo and bops him across his face with the Vactra Bopper. He swings back around and punches him in the stomach. He stops and starts laughing.* Told ya!

POGO. *He speaks in his unidentifiable accent.* You're stealing my glory. *He hops to the agent.* You will pay dearly for that.

AGENT REV. *His eyes go wide.* Uh-oh. *An arm blaster materializes on his left arm, and he fires an energy blast at the bouncing villain.*

Pogo is hit and flies backward, crashing into the ceramic wall next to the escalator.

Agent Z is avoiding Max's punches. He is playing with him, moving swiftly with a slight grin. He stops playing around, materializes a Vactra Bopper on his right hand, and punches in his stomach. Max falls to the ground.

AGENT REV. *He shouts.* I tag him now?

AGENT Z. *He is smiling while looking at Max, who is still on the ground.* Yes, you can, Rev!

AGENT REV. Heheh! Yes! *He materializes V-Cuffs.*

The young agent throws V-Cuffs at Pogo, who is already close to him. They smack him in his face and then wrap around him, immobilizing him. Max quickly pulls out a taser blade and shocks the agent in his leg and Z screams. Max stands up, shoves Z, and runs over to the tracks.

A train is approaching. Max pockets the taser blade and pulls out a vial containing sarin nerve gas.

The train is seven seconds from passing, and it's an express train and doesn't stop at this station.

Max throws the vial on the ground, and the vapors start to fill the air. The train is speeding past, and the deranged man grabs onto the train somehow, and the train is gone.

AGENT Z. *He screams out.* Rev! Activate your V-Haler!! *The V-Haler mask covers his mouth and nose.*

The younger agent is confused and panicking. Z throws a V-Shield at Pogo's immobilized body, quickly races to Rev's location, and places his hands over his mouth and nose. He has a tight hold. Z's flight board materializes and flies toward him. He jumps up (with Rev). The board glides under their boots and takes them out of the subway station.

Once they're outside, Z drops Rev, now wearing the V-Haler mask. Z materializes an Invisi-Dome and throws it in the air, and it traps them and covers the subway entrance. The Invisi-Dome expel harmful chemicals out of its dome and destroys them. Z jumps on his board and flies back inside the subway station.

The V-Shield disappears. Z grabs an immobilized Pogo and pulls him out of the subway station. He drops Pogo and lands beside Rev. Before Pogo can hit the ground, he's transported to Primous Facility.

AGENT REV. Is the psycho guy dead, Z?

AGENT Z. *He shakes his head.* Nope. I don't know how, but he escaped. He was planning to have Pogo killed.

AGENT REV. That isn't very good.

AGENT Z. Mhm. Come on. Let's get back to HQ.

The agents teleport to VLORs. Meanwhile, at VICE HQ, Floral is walking on the second level. She stops by the employee's cafeteria next to the Infirmary Ward and hears Dr. Mache and Mr. Casey's conversation.

CAMERON CASEY. *He's sitting at the round table with an empty plate and a glass of scotch.* So sad to hear about Talgitx's departure.

DR. MACHE. *He sips his green tea.* Have you heard what happened?

CAMERON CASEY. Of course! He fought Xavier and lost. *He shakes his head.* The old man isn't the same after he injured his right shoulder.

DR. MACHE. *He shakes his head.* Tragic. *He sips his tea.* Xavier looks different from the leader type.

CAMERON CASEY. And the same implies to that imbecile lover boy Delpro've. *He holds in his laughter.* He managed to do one thing right.

DR. MACHE. What was that?

CAMERON CASEY. He turned his sickly daughter into a god-awful freak of nature! Who the hell is she now, Mother Nature?

DR. MACHE. I forgot Delpro've was in line for Commander of VICE before he mysteriously went away.

CAMERON CASEY. *He snickers while drinking his scotch.* It was easy to get him out of here.

Floral tears up in the hall and quietly runs to her quarters, and she cannot hear anymore.

The door slides open, she runs in, jumps on her bed, snatches the picture of her father off the nightstand, and cries herself to sleep.

Later that night, Zhariah is sitting on the roof above the orphanage. She is crying because she heard that her friend did not make it.

It's night out, and the street lights on Tarainound Street are very bright. The girl is on the orphanage's top roof, sitting in the fetal position. Zhariah starts crying more, mourning over an excellent friend. She gazes up at the moon with tears streaming down her face.

ZHARIAH. *She talks to the moon.* Why me? *Sniffs.* Why is it always me? *She's hurting. She feels her heart is breaking apart.* I try. I d— do. I— w— wish I had someone— someone nice to remain in my life.

Little Maya opened the orphanage's back entrance to bring Zhariah inside for dinner. The child steps over the threshold, trying to locate her big sister on the roof.

MAYA. Zari? *Her voice gets louder.* Zaaaariiii?

ZHARIAH. I'm coming. *She quickly wipes away her tears using her shirt and her bare arms.*

MAYA. *Shouts.* Zari?!

ZHARIAH. *She gets to her feet, jumps down to the lower part of the roof then jumps to the ground.* I'm right here, Maya.

MAYA. *She was facing the wrong side, and she turned her body.* Zari! *She takes six fast-walking steps to her.* Mama said come and eat. *She looks into her eyes.* Why were you crying? *She becomes worried.* What's wrong?

ZHARIAH. I'm all right, and it's nothing. Thank You. *She places her left arm around the girl's neck, kisses her cheek, and walks inside.*

Season 2, Episode 13 – Rifts

Friday, June 30, 2107

The next day, in the afternoon, Cameron Casey is at Chainberland's coffeehouse in Dowers City, finishing his lunch. He looks up as the electricity at the coffeehouse, and other businesses in the area goes out.

CAMERON CASEY. *He looks down the street.* Well, what do we have here? *He notices sparks coming from a nearby alley, and he smiles and goes to check it out.*

The man peeks around the corner and sees a young boy wearing odd clothing and goggles. The boy is in deep meditation, facing the other way. The man pulls out his taser blade and slowly walks closer.

Mr. Casey was now ten steps away; the boy knew someone was in the alley with him. He moves his foot forward a little bit, and the man reaches forward, pointing his taser blade. The boy gets a tiny negative shock of electricity.

SHOCKER. *He screams and leans forward.* Ah!!!! *He turns his head and looks terrified.*

CAMERON CASEY. *He smiles.* Well, hello, cross-human. *He goes in for another attack with his taser blade.*

The boy falls to avoid the taser blade and extends his foot up, hoping to kick him. Mr. Casey jumps back to prevent his foot from making contact. Shocker rolls on the ground, getting away from him. The man pursues and shocks him several times. The boy is in pain, screaming out, and manages to use the brick wall coming up to stand. Shocker delivers a roundhouse kick, but Casey leans back and then launches forward, swiping the taser blade. The boy grabs his right wrist, twists it, and pushes him into the brick wall. He lets him go and takes off running, leaving the alley. The man turns, flicks his hair out of his face, and chases after him.

Shocker is running away, wishing he could turn his body into electricity so he can escape easily. Mr. Casey's gaining on him.

Suddenly, a jet flies over their heads and drops two pods. The man stops running as the jet vanishes. Statistabots emerge from the pods, eighty in all. The bots land, all facing him.

MR. CASEY. *He stares.* Well.

The statistabots wait for five seconds, then turn around and go after Shocker. MR. Casey is worried for a second and runs behind them, and Floral is hiding nearby.

Meanwhile, Shocker is running for his life. Suddenly, a bot shoots lightning at him. Agent Z appears on his flight board and blocks the attack using the bottom of his board. The attack redirects to the group of statistabots and takes out some of them.

The agent smiles and flies toward the rest. Z jumps off his disappearing flight board and lands on the ground. He materializes his blade and charges at the bots, attacking them one by one.

Shocker looks at Agent Z and then spots Mr. Casey running toward him. He gets scared and starts to turn around to escape. He bumps into Rahz. She was standing in that spot for a while. She looks at him. Mr. Casey ignores the girl's presence as he reaches the boy. Once he is close, Mr. Casey raises his taser blade high. At that moment, Rahz makes a quick decision. She speeds at him, grabs his arm, and punches him in his chest using a Vactra Bopper. The man flies backward about thirty feet. He knocks out three statistabots that were about to attack Z.

Three seconds later, Casey gets to his feet. Z appears and punches him in his chest multiple times and roundhouse kicks him twice. He falls.

Four statistabots are making their way to Agent Z. The boy runs at them and swipes his blade at every last one.

Rahz is now ignoring Shocker and helps Z to defeat the bots. Shocker is tired from all the running, but he toughs it out and helps beat the statistabots.

Casey is having difficulty standing up. He manages to stand, but Z spots him trying to escape. Before Z had time to act, Rahz glides past using the hover ability in her boots and attaches V-Cuffs on him. Casey is immobilized.

AGENT Z. Oh yeah!! *He says excitedly, then continues fighting the remaining bots.*

Four minutes later, Z has a chance to glance at Rahz. She is acting more aggressively than usual, but Z shakes it off, assuming she is having an off day. Suddenly, all the statistabots disappear.

AGENT Z. What th—

Shocker is breathing heavily, with his hands on his knees and looking at the ground.

AGENT Z. *He looks at his fellow agent.* Please Rahz. He did help us. Please?

She closes her eyes, stares at the clouds, and sighs. She teleports away. Shocker nods his head and quickly runs away on foot, running behind two tall buildings, and disappears.

AGENT Z. *He watches Shocker escape and smiles.* Thank you, Rahz.

Z materializes an Invisi-Dome and throws it high, and it blankets the entire area and works its magic. He watches as the immobilized Casey's transported to Gowdon's Prison. The boy teleports to HQ, and the Invisi-Dome disappears.

A bush nearby shakes many times, unusually, and Floral crawls out. She gets to her feet and dusts herself off.

FLORAL. *Smiling.* Yes! My plan worked! *She starts giggling then she teleports away from the area.*

Monday, July 03, 2107

A few days passed, Xavier walked through Drekal Park. He feels relaxed as he walks over to the trashcan and throws the empty water bottle away. He decides to exit the park and walk behind the convenience store, where his car is parked. He gets inside and drives away.

DiLusion is standing inside a warehouse located in Valousse City, Illinois. Xavier arrives at the location, and the strange man looks at him. The VICE commander walks closer and stops on DiLusion's left, and DiLusion turns around.

DILUSION. You're late, Commander Xavier.

CO. XAVIER. Oh, save it.

Xavier looks at Dr. Mache, who works with three unknown and unnamed scientists. They are standing by a gigantic computer beside a normal-sized satellite.

DILUSION. *He looks at the scientists working, and he speaks to Xavier.* Your team is quite intelligent.

CO. XAVIER. *He keeps his eyes on the lead scientist, waits five seconds, and then speaks.* Dr. Mache.

DR. MACHE. *He turns around, faces Xavier, then turns around and continues working.* How's everything, commander?

CO. XAVIER. It couldn't be better. How's everything going?

DR. MACHE. Everything is going as planned—only a few more hours.

CO. XAVIER. *He nods his head.* Excellent, Dr. Mache. *He turns to face DiLusion.* You see. Don't worry about my end. You make sure your abilities are up to par with— *He points—that* satellite.

DILUSION. My abilities work.

CO. XAVIER. *He smiles, turns, and walks toward the exit. He walks to his vehicle, gets inside, and drives away.*

DILUSION. *Thinks.* How can a human be so terrifying? *He laughs and turns around, facing Mache and the other scientists. He teleports away seconds later.*

Tuesday, July 04, 2107

On his way home, Zadarion gets a call from VLORs.

ZADARION. *He sighs.* I knew this was too good to be true, and I almost finished the day without fighting any baddies! *He seeks someplace deserted, and he teleports to VLORs.*

The boy makes it to HQ and finds Rahz in the operations room.

AGENT Z. *He steps inside, looking at her.* Hey Rahz. I was like enjoying our day off.

AGENT RAHZ. *Although she wants to agree, she doesn't feel like smiling.* Well, we're here now. *She turns her head, looking away.*

Z becomes silent. The commander's voice speaks over the intercom.

CO. ADDAMS. What are you guys doing here? *He apologizes.* I am sorry. I should have told you to head down to Valora Docks instead of coming here.

AGENT Z. *He has a concerned look on his face.* But why, sir? What's going on?

CO. ADDAMS. A colossal satellite extended up into the sky over Valousse City. Get over there now!

AGENT Z. Aye, aye!

Rahz has her head low, looking at the floor.

AGENT Z. *He turns to the girl and taps her shoulder.* Let's go, Rahz. *He exits the room making his way to the Geared'NReady Room to teleport.*

The girl raises her head and follows. Moments later, the two teleport to Valora Docks. Caj arrives at Valora Docks first.

AGENT CAJ. *He is facing the warehouse, standing in the parking lot. He spots Xavier and DiLusion at the scene.* Since when did you two become besties?

Agents Z and Rahz teleport beside him. Z gets on his left, and Rahz stands on his right.

CO. XAVIER. *He whispers to DiLusion.* After you. *He is smiling.*

DILUSION. Oh! How kind of you. *He looks at the three agents.*

XAVIER. You do that. *He raises his right arm, wearing a thin-rubber bracelet, and snaps his fingers.*

Statistabots fly out of the warehouse and make their way to the agents. DiLusion gets out of the way.

DILUSION. *He gets out of the way.* Clever. *He looks at Xavier.*

XAVIER. I have important matters to attend.

DILUSION. *He raises his voice.* No, you do—

The agents are fighting the statistabots.

AGENT CAJ. *He slices two bots with his arm blades.* Wow. Look at the married couple disagreeing.

The female agent is quietly fighting statistabots.

AGENT Z. *He punches three bots using the Vactra Bopper and starts laughing hysterically, but mostly only to taunt the fused scientist.*

DiLusion listens to the laughter, and it gets to him. He disappears into a portal. He reappears behind Z and kicks him in his back. The boy falls to the ground. The man disappears again. Caj closes his eyes. DiLusion reappears behind the teenager. Caj turns around, opens his eyes, and kicks him in his chest. The man falls, but a portal opens under him, and he disappears.

Four bots fly toward a distracted Z, and the boy rolls away and manages to stand. The four bots turn and go after him, and Rahz zooms past and shoots all four with her blaster.

AGENT Z. Thanks.

The girl passes Z, looks at him, and zooms toward the remaining bots. A portal starts opening on the ground, and Rahz approaches it unknowingly as DiLusion creeps out. The boy activates the hovering ability in his boots and zooms to the opening portal. He dives in front of the girl about to be attacked and goes into the portal.

It closes and reopens in the sky above. The two fall out and land on the ground, and the portal closes. DiLusion is standing. Caj comes out of nowhere and knees him in his chest. Z stands up, does a roundhouse kick, and kicks him across his face. The boy returns to materialize his blaster and shoots the man in his chest. Caj grabs hold of his right arm. Z jumps in the air and aims at DiLusion in a high jump kick. The man quickly grabs Caj's arm and reverses their position. Z kicks Caj in his chest, and DiLusion punches Z. Caj manages to pull DiLusion down. Rahz speeds in close and shoots the man with her blaster. He falls and lands on his teleporting device, and it gets damaged.

DILUSION. No. No. No!! *He stands up.* You didn't!!

Caj and Z stand up, focusing their attention on DiLusion.

AGENT CAJ. Yeah! Now that's teamwork! *He is smiling.* Without that, let's see how you deal. *He gets ready to attack.*

DILUSION. *He is angry.* I don't have to *deal,* you smart-mouthed juvenile!

AGENT Z. *He is laughing.* We made him mad. *He is ready to fight, and he is holding his blade the wrong way.*

DILUSION. *He starts grinning.* I've distracted you long enough.

AGENT RAHZ. *She walks closer to her fellow agents after finishing off the remaining statistabots.* What does that mean?

The satellite activates. The three agents look to the sky, and DiLusion is also watching. Xavier walks outside, approaching the fused scientist.

CO. XAVIER. *He stops and stands close to him.* You're up.

The fused man takes the device off his wrist, channels his ability, and extends his right arm out, and the broken machine starts glowing.

AGENT CAJ. I'm not going to watch this. *He charges in.*

CO. XAVIER. *He grabs his right arm before he makes contact with DiLusion.* Don't be rude. *He knees him in the stomach and throws him to the ground.*

The teenager gets to his feet and aims at Xavier. He blocked every last of Caj's attempts to cut him using his arm blades. The teenager is persistent and manages to punch him in the face. The man pauses for five seconds while looking at the ground.

AGENT CAJ. *He starts grinning.* Not so tough after all.

CO. XAVIER. Heh.

The VICE commander tries punching Caj but blocks it using his left arm. Xavier comes back, grabs his left arm, flips him on the ground, picks him up, and throws him into the closest light pole, and Caj smacks into it.

Z gets angry and charges in, and so does Rahz. Xavier stays where he is and waits. The teens reach their target. Z goes in low and throws a punch, and Rahz throws a punch in his face. The man grabs both their fists. The boy pulls away, but Xavier slams him into Rahz, and they fall to the ground—the two stand.

CO. XAVIER. Oh! Want more?

The teens come in from different angles. Xavier avoids them. He roundhouse kicks Z because he is the closest, and he hits the ground hard. Rahz throws a punch, and Xavier sidesteps, grabs her arm, and flips her over his left shoulder. She falls on her back.

At this time, DiLusion already threw his broken teleporting device at the satellite. The satellite is starting to create a wormhole, and Xavier looks at it enlarging. Five seconds later, the wormhole begins to spark, becoming unstable. Caj aims his blaster and shoots at it three times.

DILUSION. *He looks at the teenager.* No!!!!

The wormhole is reacting, and it shrinks. The satellite is giving off sparks. A white beam of light shoots from the active satellite and opens a portal across from it. The satellite breaks into tiny pieces. This new portal resembles DiLusion's portals.

AGENT Z. *He is looking at the sky and is astonished.* What have they done?

Ten seconds later, the fully opened portal creates a vacuum effect, pulling everything inside.

AGENT CAJ. *He shouts.* Z, Rahz! Grab hold of something!!!! *He grabs onto the light pole.*

The VLORs trio quickly starts to grab onto whatever is near them. Xavier and DiLusion have special locking devices built into their shoes, locking to the concrete.

What Rahz holds onto starts to give in; she's aiming for it and screaming.

AGENT Z. *He shouts while his eyes follow a terrified Rahz.* No!!!! *He lets go of the street pole.*

The portal's force is pulling him faster. Quickly thinking, he pulls out a skinny and strong V-Line rope, and Z throws it out toward Rahz as he passes her. The line wraps around her leg twice. He activates the magnetizing mechanism by twisting the thin line and attaching it to a Tripcoin, which can change its weight. Z throws the coin as hard as he can because the pull force on his body is too much for him to resist. It hits the ground, and the boy materializes his blaster and shoots the ground where DiLusion and Xavier are standing.

Caj is holding onto a light pole tightly, and he uses one hand to position his blaster where DiLusion and Xavier are both standing. Unknowingly, at the same time as Z, he shoots his blaster, and both lasers hit the concrete under their feet—the concrete cracks. Z is now inside the portal. Within five seconds, so are DiLusion and Xavier.

Right after the portal pulls in the three humans, it becomes much more unstable and starts to close. At this moment, light forcibly shoots out, and the stream of light is so thin no one notices. It strikes a building in the area, forming a person. This new being is kneeling, stands up, opens his eyes, and admires his new BIO-Being flesh.

CURDUR. *He grins.* It's good that I stored a sufficient number of these things in a virtual space dumpster. *He laughs.*

Wednesday, July 05, 2107

The next day, Curdur is out again; this time, Agent Z is nowhere on Earth.

Curdur is in Hidendale Springs trying to find him so he can rechallenge him.

CURDUR. *He is walking down Tarainound Street in his unusual attire.* Where are you hiding, my doppelganger?

After a couple of failures to lure him out, he senses, within himself, that he's gone.

CURDUR. *He stops walking and quietly thinks to himself, crossing his arms.* It's weird because I am alive; he must be alive somewhere. But where?

The feeling he's getting is that the agent never existed. He comes up with an idea and uncrosses his arms.

CURDUR. Well. I guess it's time to do some re-evaluation of his so-called life. *He grins evilly and continues walking.* Wherever you are, once you return, you'll have nothing! *He stops grinning.* Hm. I could use a change of clothing.

After walking through Hidendale Springs for a few minutes, Curdur flies to Valousse City. He lands on the roof of the Marwolon department store. He walks down the stairwell, exits the double doors, and enters the hall. He locates a clothing store and walks inside.

Curdur looks around, getting a lot of stares because of his clothing. He decides to ignore the few people for now. After five minutes of searching through clothes, he walks to a fitting room carrying a lot of clothes.

CURDUR. Time to become a complete replica of the real Zadarion! *He smiles deviously and enters a fitting room.*

He is inside trying on several items. He looks in the mirror and decides to switch it up.

Fifteen minutes later…

UNNAMED SALESPERSON. *She knocks on the door.* First, we appreciate your business with us and seek to make our customers comfortable. So, how are the selections you've chosen to try on?

CURDUR. *He thinks to himself.* Ugh. Annoying. *He fakes a pleasurable attitude.* You're adorable. Everything's fabulous!

UNNAMED SALESPERSON. *She hears another customer entering the store.* Well, thank you. Let me know if you need any additional assistance. *She's going to greet the other customer.*

After shopping at several clothing stores around the city, he spent a few hours getting familiar with the area, starting with Zadarion's friends and practicing perfecting his personality and mannerisms.

It is now eight o'clock in the evening. He entered Jones's residence and successfully tricked Mrs. Jones but not Kiley. He entered Zada's room and fell asleep.

Thursday, July 06, 2107

The following day, Zadarion wakes up in his bed, eats breakfast, and leaves for school.

It's starting to be a long day. He almost suffocates his face inside a textbook because he is so bored. The bell rings for the end of the second period.

ZADARION. *He thinks.* Why do they need to learn this crap? *He shakes his head and walks to his locker.*

An hour later, the boy is in his Intro to Foreign Language class. He walks out to go to the restroom, and he takes his backpack with him.

ZADARION. Lunch is approaching soon. I wonder how their food tastes.

He is dangling his backpack in his left hand, walking from his foreign language class, and heading to the restroom. He is down the hall on the other side of the building. Dave Mikaelson is walking down another hall, which intersects the passageway Zadarion is currently roaming.

Dave is fresh out of the juvenile detention center in Melaro Village, Indiana. He is looking for someone to take his frustrations out on because it's been too long since he last bullied someone.

Zadarion passes in front of him, heading down the hallway for the restroom. He sees Zadarion and remembers where they left off and follows him. The teenager runs down the hall, turns the corner, and runs to the teen.

DAVE MIKAELSON. *He shouts.* Hey, prick!!

The teen keeps walking. He hears someone shouting but does not recognize the person's voice, so he continues walking. Dave catches up to him, stops running, and grabs his shoulder. Zadarion stops walking but does not look at him.

DAVE MIKAELSON. *He walks in front of him.* I got to say. I missed you, buddy. *He cracks his knuckles.* So. Are we gon' finish where we left off? Heh. Yeah.

ZADARION. *He does not bother looking in his direction, and his eyes look straight ahead.* Excuse me. *He raises his arm to move him out of the way.*

Dave stares at him with confusion on his face. Zadarion walks on, and he goes into the boy's restroom.

DAVE MIKAELSON. *He shouts at the door.* All right. Pretend you don't know me! *He shakes his head and whispers.* I'll get you after school. *He walks away. He sees kids staring at him.* What are you looking at? *He pushes an unknown young boy against his locker and keeps walking.*

Zhariah witnessed the whole thing. She is standing in front of the girl's restroom with a book in front of her face, pretending to be reading. She is doubting this Zadarion. His facial expressions looked familiar, but she could not put two and two together. She walks down the hallway like she is not being nosy.

Zadarion is in the restroom, washing his hands. He dries his hands and looks at his reflection in the mirror.

ZADARION. I make this look good. *He chuckles.*

The teen leaves the restroom. After the door closed, Alec exited the stall where he was hiding.

ALEC. *He is looking very concerned.* Zada. Was that you?

As Zadarion steps out of the restroom, he bumps into Jayla and Kiyla.

JAYLA. Excuuuuuuse you, Zada. *She retorts.*

ZADARION. Chill female. *He continues walking.*

KIYLA. What did he say? *She is stunned.*

JAYLA. He called me female. *She needs clarification.*

KIYLA. I've only known him for a short time, and that's odd to me too.

JAYLA. Let's go to lunch, Kiyla.

The time is ten minutes to three in the evening. The end of the school day is vastly approaching. Dave is looking at Zadarion from the back of the class. The teen boy is sitting at his desk, looking out the window. Dave is just waiting for the bell to ring so that he can deal with him.

Ten minutes later...

The time is now three o'clock in the evening. The school bell rings, and all students flood the hallways, gathering their belongings.

Zadarion uses his fist and gently taps his locker to open it. Dave is making his way to the teen's locker. Zadarion grabs his things out of his locker, stowing away his books, then closes his locker. Dave is now standing behind him. Zadarion turns around and sees him looking rather upset.

ZADARION. *He looks at Dave, and then he looks at the floor.* Can you please move?

DAVE MIKAELSON. *He pushes him against his locker.* Listen punk! I don't know who you think you are talking to, but we gon' squash all this right now! *He resembles a blowfish right now.*

A horde of students is now surrounding them. Zhariah was about to exit the school, but she heard the students making a commotion, so she walked toward the crowd of people. Alec is in the middle of the mass of people.

ZADARION. *He whispers to Dave.* Do I know you, blowfish?

DAVE MIKAELSON. *He grabs his T-shirt and pins him against his locker. He shouts.* Shut up!!!!

ZADARION. *He is grinning.* Right. Heh. Note to self. Don't mention blowfish again. *He waits for a few seconds, then punches the teenager in his chest.*

Dave gasps for air and has no choice but to let go of his T-shirt, taking three steps back. All the students surrounding them become surprised.

Zadarion starts pacing with a smirk. Dave looks up at him.

DAVE MIKAELSON. *He is holding his chest because there's pain.* You're– so dead. *He starts to come to the teen.*

Zadarion jumps and kicks away from his locker, punching Dave. The force of the teen's punch causes the bully to fly toward the lockers on the other side of the hallway and smack into the lockers. The crowd of students look surprised.

ZADARION. *He walks over to him and bends down to his level.* Do you want some more? *He laughs.*

The teen boy stands up tall, looking down at the bully. Dave is on the ground, hurting, but he tries to pull himself up using the lockers. The teenager grabs the teen boy's shirt, and Zadarion punches him. The right side of Dave's face hit the locker behind him. Zadarion chuckles.

With a sixth sense, the teen boy hears someone wearing dress shoes approaching and takes two steps back.

Dave is pissed off and refuses to let a pipsqueak punk embarrass him. He gets to his feet and successfully punches the boy in his face. Zadarion falls to the floor, holding his seemingly throbbing face. The principal enters through the crowd of students.

PRINCIPAL HARVIEL. Okay, Mr. Dave. That's it! *He grabs his right arm.* Back to school, and you're already picking on someone. Let's go to my office. *He walks him through the crowd of students.* You, students, go home now! *He shouted.*

Dave turns his head to look at the teen boy on the floor. Zadarion is getting to his feet, staring back. He winks and smiles. Dave turns his head, looking somewhat disappointed.

The crowd of students disperses. Alec walks into a nearby classroom, and Zhariah is standing behind the group of students. When the students spread, she saw an unusual look on Zadarion's face. She grips her book bag tight and lowers her eyes to the floor.

Zadarion chuckles, grabs his book bag and walks toward the exit. Zhariah watches him while standing at the side of the hallway. The teen boy walks out of the exit doors.

Five minutes later, he walks down Tarainound Street with his book bag over his right shoulder. He crosses the street, and a car nearly runs him over. The driver abruptly stops his car in front of him and sticks his head out his window.

UNNAMED CAR DRIVER. Hey kid. *He shouts.* Move out of the way!
  He said with attitude.

The boy turns his head, turns his body, and stares at him. He drops his book bag and grimaces at the driver. The man sticks his head back in his car, gripping the steering wheel.

Zadarion raises his right fist and slams his fist into the front of the man's car. He pulls his hand out. There's a massive dent in the car. You can see the engine. The man is terrified. Zadarion chuckles. The man tries to get out of his car to flee. The boy walks to the driver's side of the vehicle. A force comes out of nowhere, and something scoops him off his feet and takes him far away.

An invisible tornado, acting as an Invisi-Dome, was activated once Zada left the scene. The man in the car forgets what he just witnessed. He exits his car, looks around, looks at his damaged vehicle, and assumes he was involved in a hit-and-run.

Far from the previous location, Zadarion falls in the middle of Drekel Park, and an Invisi-Dome surrounds the entire area. The boy stands and looks around, smiling, and a girl stands in front of him.

ZADARION. What's up, Rahz? Why are you doing this to me?

AGENT RAHZ. Cut the act, Curdur.

ZADARION. I don't know what you're— *He stares at her.*

AGENT RAHZ. *She materializes her daggers.* It's over.

CURDUR. Heh. Okay. You caught me. So you're going to bring me in? *He chuckles.*

AGENT RAHZ. What did you do with Agent Z?

CURDUR. I haven't done anything. Oh, wait. Let me change out of these ridiculous-looking clothes. *He snaps his fingers. The programming of the BIO-Beings enables him to change what he is wearing digitally. After two seconds, he's in the same attire as when he first appeared.* That's better. *He grins.* I'm waiting.

Rahz throws her right hand back and then swipes her dagger out in front of her. Lightning comes from it and is about to hit him.

CURDUR. *He side-steps to the right and avoids the attack. He looks at his clothing and dusts himself off.* You gon' have to do better than that. *He's punched across his face.*

The girl starts swiping her daggers at him. Curdur pulls his body back and throws his right foot out in front of him. She uses the flight ability in her boots and flies in the air. Curdur looks into the sky, points his arm blaster, and fires three attacks at her.

The girl is in the air, looking down at him. Curdur's attacks are coming in fast, aiming at her. She flies away from them. The three attacks miss. Curdur jumps high, aiming at her. She throws her left leg at his head. The imposter raises his left arm to block her kick. He jabs his right hand at her stomach. She barely escaped, twisting her body and spinning to the ground, landing on her feet. She rubs her belly. Curdur grazed her. The imposter intentionally falls to the ground, landing a few feet away.

CURDUR. You're good for a female. *He laughs.*

AGENT RAHZ. Heh. *She de-materializes her daggers.*

Curdur charges at her. The girl leans to the right and punches him across his face. Curdur looks at her, smiles, and hits Rahz in her chest. The force of his punch causes her to fly backward, and she keeps herself from falling by doing a backflip.

Curdur rushes at her and throws a punch. She sidesteps to her right and kicks out in front of her. The clone jumps a little off the ground to avoid her kick, but Rahz punches him in his stomach. Curdur lands on the ground, holding his midsection. The girl flips over him and throws a punch. Curdur grabs her right arm and throws her over his shoulder. She rolls on the ground. The clone goes after her and starts stomping the ground as she moves. She stops, shielding her face and stomach. The girl discreetly taps a button on her V-Link, emitting a pulse. The short burst of sound immobilizes Curdur for a few seconds. He covers his ears.

Rahz gets to her feet and starts punching him multiple times. She materializes the Vactra Boppers and repeats her attacks.

Curdur's taking multiple hits. He reaches for her Vactra Boppers and successfully grabs both of them, preventing her from continuing her attacks. He prepares to kick Rahz. The girl flips over Curdur's head and throws him in the air. It happened so fast. Curdur was surprised, so he let go of the Vactra Boppers. He stops midair and shoots his body downward like a rocket. His body hit the ground where she was standing before she flipped out of the way. Dust fills the area. Curdur runs after her and starts throwing punches.

CURDUR. Fight like a man, get dealt with like a man! *He throws his left leg.*

The girl raises her right arm to block, but she's knocked to the ground. He stands over her, grinning.

Caj appears and swings his left leg at his head. He turns his head because he hears a force coming at him from behind. The clone allows it and falls on his face. He rolls on his back and smiles at the newcomer.

CURDUR. Heh. The big man is here!

Caj stomps the ground where Curdur is lying. The clone grabs his foot and twists it. The teenager's body twirls in the air. Curdur lets go of his foot, stands up, and gets ready to punch him. Rahz appears and hits Curdur in the back of his head. Curdur does a roundhouse kick and kicks her. She falls to the ground, but she gets back up.

The agents are both eyeing him. Caj stands in front of him, and Rahz stands behind him.

CURDUR. *He turns around to face the girl.* Heh.

AGENTS CAJ. *He runs closer to the clone, and his body disappears.*

CURDUR. Oh boy! Tricks!

The ground loosens under Curdur's feet, and Caj starts to emerge. The clone quickly jumps back and grabs Caj's arm from the ground at lightning speed. He uses his strength and throws him high in the air. He quickly extends his arm blaster and fires multiple shots, all of which hit Caj. Smoke fills the area.

AGENT RAHZ. Caj!!!!!

AGENT CAJ. I'm right here! *He is walking behind the girl agent, holding his left arm.* I'm okay. It was a copy.

CURDUR. Aw. *He says teasingly.* I'll make sure next time I'll grab the real you. *He winks his left eye.*

AGENT CAJ. There won't be a next time.

The girl agent teleports and reappears in the sky above the clone.

CURDUR. There's something unique about you, and I'm sensing darkness inside you.

The girl materializes one of her daggers, shoots down like a rocket, and attempts to slash his chest.

CURDUR. Even I know when I'm defeated. *He laughs and disappears. He avoids her attack.*

The girl slows her speed and safely falls to the ground, landing on the ground. She looks around, expecting a sneak attack. A minute later, nothing comes, and Caj walks closer to her.
AGENT CAJ. He ran because he couldn't take the two of us.

The two agents teleport back to HQ.

Friday, August 04, 2107

A few weeks later, the end of the summer semester for Centransdale High School comes to an end. A new family, a father and daughter, arrive at their new home in Hidendale Springs, Illinois.

After they finish admiring their new house, Valery asks her father if it's okay to visit the local mall. Her father agrees, but only if she brings back some of the local food because he is starving. The girl's stomach growls when he mentions food, and she smiles and walks out the door.

The girl is walking down Tarainound Street and decides to cut through an alley, making her way to see the local mall in the area.

Suddenly, someone falls out of the sky and crashes into a dumpster. Valery dives behind a trashcan, peeks her head out, and stares. She sees a teen boy get off the ground and dust himself off. She starts blushing and continues looking at him.

ZADARION. *He sighs.* Yes! I made it back! *He checks his V-Link.* Thank you. It's working again! I have to get to HQ! *He transforms into his agent attire, and he teleports to VLORs.*

VALERY. *She watches in amazement.* He's awesome! *She blinks three times fast.* And cute. *She takes slow deep breaths.* What is this I'm feeling? *She snaps out of it and looks for the boy.*

The girl sees no one.

There are trash bags behind her, and she is kneeling behind a trash can. A homeless man rises from the trash bags.

UNNAMED HOMELESS PERSON. Hello there. Why, what are you doing in an alley like this?

She hears a strange man talking behind her. Valery turns her head to the side, seeing the homeless man looking at her pervertedly. She's showing no expression. The girl turns her head away from him and stands up tall. She raises her leg behind her, kicking the man in his face.

The man is now unconscious. The girl continues on her way to go check out the local mall.

Meanwhile, VLORs operators picked up Agent Z's signal and sent the coordinates to Agent Caj. He teleports to the coordinates sent to him. He rushes to the scene, finds no one, and teleports to VLORs.

After stopping by his house and secretly checking on everyone, Z teleports to VLORs. He is now inside the Geared'NReady room and makes his way to the operations room. Rahz comes out of the room fully concealed and sees him walking toward the operations room. She thinks she spotted Curdur, and she attacks him. Z tries to fight her off. Rahz is hell-bent on killing Curdur for good. She is acting more violently than usual.

AGENT Z. Rahz. It's me! Agent Z!

AGENT RAHZ. You're not fooling me, Curdur!

AGENT Z. *He pushes Rahz back.* Rahz, I swear. Something happened! I am back now! Tell me, how and when did Curdur come back?

AGENT RAHZ. *She charges at him. Shouts.* Stop lying!!!!

A V-Cuff flies at Z from behind, wrapping around and immobilizing him. Z's body falls to the floor. Rahz stops running, looks at an immobilized Z, then looks at the approaching people.

AGENT CAJ. *He walks closer to the boy's immobilized body.* We got him.

CO. ADDAMS. *He is walking closer.* Which one is this?

AGENT CAJ. Sir, this is the counterpart, Curdur.

AGENT RAHZ. *She is looking at the immobilized boy.*

CO. ADDAMS. Where's your proof?

AGENT CAJ. I have to get back to you on that one, sir.

AGENT RAHZ. *She walks closer, gets down on one knee, and lifts his right sleeve. Her eyes go wide, and she stands up tall. It's Agent Z. She turns around and faces Commander Addams.*

CO. ADDAMS. How do you know precisely?

AGENT RAHZ. During our first fight with Curdur behind Hidendale Observatory, I never saw the metallic armband on Curdur's right arm.

Caj and Addams look at Z's right arm. They are shocked.

CO. ADDAMS. Very observant.

AGENT CAJ. Yeah. Very nice.

They carry Z to the operations room. Addams wants to know what happened to him and where he's been for the past few weeks.

Saturday, August 05, 2107

The next day, after checking in with VLORs, Z decides to take a trip to a secluded island, Chribale Isle. This island is small and uninhabited, well as of two days ago.

He teleports to the island by tapping into the mysterious powers in the metallic device on his right arm.

AGENT Z. It's weird how my right t-shirt sleeve goes under this mysterious armband. Shouldn't it cover it? Hm. *He ignores what he is talking to himself about, checks his V-Link, and notices it isn't working correctly. He whispers.* Yes. I have about an hour before VLORs can track my location. *He looks ahead and walks further, passing by many trees.*

He walks further until he cannot go any farther. He locates a cave-like hole leading underground. He steps inside, walks a few steps, and stops.

AGENT Z. *He speaks softly.* I know you're there, SciQui. *He stands in the dark cave and waits for a reply.*

SCIQUI. *He opens his eyes, and they're glowing. There's a white light coming from them.* It is fascinating running into you again.

AGENT Z. *He grins.* Really dude? *He is smiling.* I know you're feeling upset that I found where you landed so quickly before you could roam away.

SCIQUI. Yeah, yeah. *He pauses for a few minutes.* It's also a shame what happened to the little guy, your precious little friend, on planet Vexion. The poor little guy went all evil.

AGENT Z. *He fakes laughs.* Yeah! You just better *hope* he's not here! But you know, it's funny. You're one of several that can speak English, and I happen to locate you first! Thanks to this— *He shows the Vex-Armor emblem.*

SCIQUI. *He eyes the emblem, and he looks at him.* You were lucky to have been given such a rare item.

AGENT Z. Yeah. *He smiles a little and turns around.* I will be in touch if another Vexion creature shows up on Earth. *He starts walking out of the cave then he turns around.* Oh! And also— *He raises his right shirt sleeve.* You *will* help me figure out this strange object on my arm. You are knowledgeable about the "universe" and all. *He winks his left eyelid.* I'll be seeing you, SciQui.

Once Agent Z exits the cave, SciQui starts chuckling in his corner.

SCIQUI. *He growls and then smiles.* I will— proclaim what's rightfully mine, odd young one!

The agent reaches the end of the cave. He positions his Vex-Armor emblem directly at the cave's entrance, and it closes with an invisible shield keeping the creature from leaving and keeping everyone out. He takes off on his flight board.

Five seconds later, he receives a call on his V-Link. After the urgent call, he races to Kale County, Illinois.

Meanwhile, an older adult gets off a city bus in Valousse City, Illinois, right in front of InquiZiehion, a local newsprint and media organization also dealing with online web content. Stan Bough is the editor-in-chief. There's a tall building on the city's west side, at the corner of Seventh Street and Fifer Lane, and its most distinguishing and famous feature is the enormous silver scroll sitting at an angle on top of the building.

The elder walks closer to the building. He is in front of the InquiZiehion building and spots a taxi parking near the curb.

VICTOR MCKNIGHT. My old friend, Stan. *He is smiling.*

STAN BOUGH. *He gets out of the taxi and looks at the approaching person.* Well, if it isn't my good friend, Victory. *He closes the taxi door and walks closer to his old high school friend.*

The two shake hands and hug and walk into the building.

...to be continued

Appendix

Hidendale Springs, Illinois *Thirty minutes north of Dowers City, IL.*
- Hidendale Observatory *Home of an all new exhibit with twenty planets on display.*
- Centransdale High School
  - o *At the corner of Centransdale High School (right end of building)... you can turn left to get to Westick Blvd. There's an alley next to a convenience store.*
  - o *At the same corner of Centransdale High School... you can turn right to get to Venue Ave. If you continue walking straight, you'll reach Cuues Marketplace.*
  - o *At Centransdale High School (in between the left end and right end of the building), if you exit out of the side doors and turn right, you'll be walking away from the school (your back is now facing the school as you're walking away from it). Continue walking away from the school and you're approaching Blake Street. Continue walking straight down this street to NH Pharmacy. Continue walking, you'll pass NH Pharmacy. The next street is Valmar Street (approx. 100 steps). You're walking one hundred more steps to Florestses street. There are many shopping centers in the area.*

- Cenbaile Street *This Street cuts through Tarainound Street. It's near Remeliat Street.*
- Venue Avenue
  - o Cuues Marketplace
- Westick Boulevard
  - o Convenience Store next to an alley
  - o Centransdale High School
- Blake Street
  - o Going towards NH Pharmacy
  - o NH Pharmacy opened in the Fall of 2107.

- Valmar Street
  - o Passing NH Pharmacy
  - o Hidendale Defenders Police Headquarters. *Two floor office space, car storage garage.*
  - o Italia Ricci's Italian Guardalian Restaurant. *Two blocks from Hidendale Defenders HQ.*
- Florestses Street
  - o Many shopping centers in this area.
  - o Ion Foods *Sells nutritional snacks and your regular grocery.*
- Himswelm Street
  - o Going to Narthaniel Park District
  - o Abigail's Home for Youths Foster Care is here
  - o The corner before you reach the foster care is Qwinzale's Convenience Store
- Benjamin Weismans Boulevard *Position yourself at Kiyla Gerald's residence and from there, four blocks north from Jayla's home.*
- Remeliat Street *Intersects with Tarainound Street.*
- Tarainound Street *A main street and a really long one. This street is a one-straight shot to many restaurants, convenience stores, and many cities.*
- Drekal Park District *The closest park to Tarainound Street with many art pieces in the center of the park.*
- Narthaniel Park District *The closest park to Himswelm Street, with one walkway and a children's park.*
- Abigail's Home for Youths Foster Care *Located on Himswelm Street next to Narthaniel Park District.*
- Drenden Mountain *Located behind Hidendale Observatory.*
- Marquee Arcade *Located on Cimdal Avenue, a few blocks away from Tarainound Street. The only arcade in town, filled with a wide variety of video games, including virtual games, two-player games, and more*
- Teen Realm Media Center 'T-Realm' *A place for teens. It's located a block away from Cimdal Avenue. There's video games, fast food buffet, information counter server, free internet access, virtual televisions to watch all your favorite movies and shows.*
- Maxie's Bar & Grill *Located down the street from arcade.*

- Crumarus Hospital *Located west of Tarainound Street. The hospital is closer to Wayworth Bridge, leading to Ococo Town, Illinois.*
- HiiWell Beach *A wide beach where couples, families, and young adults come to enjoy their free schedules. There's clean waters thanks to Kale County's Newoluir's Lake that lies behind Stratum Oil Industries and MechaWaste in Dowers City, IL. Stratum Oil and MechaWaste helps to purify the water supply. Unfortunately, there's a few problems with the Diamond and Ore Okiewa Chemical factory. Sometimes, there's chemical leaks that are detected in the water's supply. There's a bit of a huge distance between. Once chemicals make contact with the small lake in Dowers City, it travels through the underwater tunnels and eventually make contact with the waters at this beach.*
- Aions Hospital
  - o *This one huge hospital. There are many patient room spaces, several offices for all higher staff member, four recreational rooms for patient recovery, two family waiting room centers filled with many forms of entertainment and prayer pamphlets, and three information centers for the three entrance zones (Zone Alpha, Bravo, and Charlie) to the hospitals. There is no entry past the information centers unless all personnel show a form of identification. They're very strict on this policy.*
  - o Room 2118, Hall E *Mr. Maxill stayed inside this room. Wealthy members stay here.*

Kale County, Illinois *Fifteen minutes south of Hidendale Springs, IL.*
- Kris Helmsdale Recreational hall
- NH Pharmacy *A smaller pharmacy compared to the others.*
- Miss Missy's Daycare *Located on Mitchel Street.*
- Governor Stephan Gunneim's place of birth
- Ion Foods *Sells nutritional snacks and your regular grocery. Ten minutes near Mitchel Street. Located on Rodabagel Avenue.*
- Iron Row Apartment Complex
- SpeedWay Rail Lines *A smaller and miniature sized train station. There's only two train services in and out of this area.*
- Stratum Oil Industries *Third office location.*

- Newoluir's Lake *lies behind Stratum Oil Industries*
- McVanders Crafts N' Supplies, INC. *Abandoned since 2089.*
- Pyro and Dyro's mother's home, Mrs. Amelia Daggerton. *On Rouche Street*
- Derick Jackson's home. *On Nathom Street, down from Iron Row Apartment Complex.*

Dowers City, Illinois *thirty minutes south of Hidendale Springs, IL.*
- VICE Secret Warehouse *This is where unnamed VICE scientists constructed many electronic emitters and the place DiLusion destroyed.*
- MechaWaste *A garbage waste and recycling separating facility.*
- Chainberland's coffeehouse *Located on Quail Street.*
- Kelo Ritz's home and secret lab. *(Local Residence)*
  o   Gravers Street
- Dale's Shopping Center *Located on Quail Street, down from 43rd street, turn left.*
  o   VicLow *A designer shoe store.*
  o   DQ's Deluxe Grocery
  o   Kang's *A fashionable, gothic and emo style clothing store.*
  o   Lu's *An expensive female clothing store. Sell dresses and stylish leggings.*
  o   Pens-R *A store selling a variety of different kinds of pens.*
  o   CinAEma *A two-room theatre. Shows current and old-school movies.*
  o   Dac 'O Noodles *A Japanese and Swedish combo restaurant.*
  o   Burger Junior *A fast food hangout spot for young adults. Sells Kids Meal's, including a burger, French fries, soda and or milkshakes.*
  o   Icy Sam's *A frozen yogurt spot.*
  o   R Ams GO *Sells a variety of designer shoes. No dress shoes.*
  o   Men's Style~House *A variety of business suits, including dress shoes.*
  o   Click-Clack Toys *Sells many different and noisy children's toys.*
  o   Ani<>More *A teen chill spot. Has toys, barbies plus action figures, and video games to sell. The public can also view the televisions, displaying commercials of the newest items soon to be on sale at the store.*

- Diamond and Ore Okiewa Chemical Factory *located in the little forest of Dowers City*
  - o There's an unnamed lake right behind this factory. It's small but under the water there's underwater tunnels connecting to Newoluir's Lake in Kale County and HiiWell Beach in Hidendale Springs, IL.
- Q National Bank *Located on 44th & Pulaski Avenue.*
- NH Pharmacy+ *A store and there's a kiosk across from it.*
- Iron Steam Factory *The employees help create reinforced iron steel for building. This is on Quail Street. This building has been repaired in the beginning of the year 2098.*

Flavrare County (Town), Illinois *fifteen minutes north of Valousse City, IL.*
- One of Kelo Ritz's homes and one of his secret laboratories *Located on Gravers Street.*
- Mackie's Donuts Store
- NH Pharmacy *A smaller pharmacy store, compared to the others.*
- Gowdon's Prison *This place houses many inmates for all sorts of crimes.*
- Lexus Street *It's near a wide, open field, just down from Mackie's Donuts Store.*
- Iris's Fashion Jewelry Store
- Ion Foods *Sells nutritional snacks and your regular grocery. 30 minutes away from Gravers Street. Located on Noturor Street.*
- SpeedWay Rail Lines *SpeedWay Rail Train going in and out of the town.*
- Vickie Male's Play Park and Art Street *A children's playground and many pathways where lots of artwork are displayed.*

Valousse City, Illinois *thirty minutes south of Dowers City, IL.*
- Lincoln Oaks Mall *A huge shopping center with great but mostly expensive stores and a very few affordable ones.*
- NH Pharmacy
  - o *A larger pharmacy. The largest one compared to the others in nearby cities. There is a plaque on the wall when you walk inside. It is the CEO, Neal Heartman. Mr. Heartman*

> *was involved in a tragic accident that cost him his life. This man dedicated his life to discovering a cure for cancer.*

- Anaheim Industries: Applied Sciences Division *Curtis Jemore Anaheim, owner and CEO*
- Lorisdale National Park *This park has trails lined with art sculptures, a center fountain, a children's playground, and a 3D walk-in house*
- Stratum Oil Industries *The Company's second office location.*
- Valora Docks *A docking port for fisherman with two warehouses for housing boats.*
- First National Bank
- InQuiZiehion
  - o *A local newsprint and media organization, also deals with online web content. Stan Bough is the editor-in-chief. This place is a tall building located on the west side of the city, at the corner of Seventh Street and Fifer Lane. The building's most distinguishing and famous feature is the enormous silver scroll sitting at an angle on top of the building.*
- Marwolon *A huge men's and women's department store.*
- Starwoks Coffee House
- Valousse Convention Center
- SpeedWay Rail Stations *SpeedWay Rail Trains going in and out of the city.*
- TechStrumm Industries *At the start of the New Year, a project was pushed forward. A sign is placed in front of the old building in January 2108 reading, "Coming Soon! Vale Corp-Industries"*
- R.Stop Tavern *Nowhere near the city. Three miles going southeast away from the city.*
- Ion Foods *Sells nutritional snacks and your regular grocery. 30 minutes from the Lincoln Oaks Mall. Located on Himole Street.*

Laroouse City, Illinois *An hour and thirty minutes west of Valousse City, IL.*
- Skyyas Airport
- SpeedWay Rail Stations *SpeedWay Rail Trains and GoRail Alpha Line, Bravo Line, and Charlie Line trains come in and out of this city from others faraway cities.*
- Nicolás el alimento *Spanish restaurant with many delicious foods. Located on Dekonkae Avenue.*

- Cromane Street *Walking away from Nicolás el alimento's Spanish restaurant.*
- Anqua Industries *An organization that finds new ways for living a comfortable life. There are many departments.*
  - o Ewellon Department *is the nation's leading competitive energy provider. The Anqua team and Ewellon staff participate in every stage of the energy business, from generation to competitive energy sales to transmission to delivery. Ewellon alone works in finding new ways to distribute electricity to various places, businesses, and residences. The president of this department, Tom Ewelling, is the creator of ELiPiP. A small device (no bigger than your average cell phone). This is a new unlimited power source that many businesses desire to have in their possession. It's clean, renewable energy. This device can receive and generate massive amounts of electricity within the programmed area.*
- Adlum Corporation
  - o *An organization that sponsors high-level corporate level campaigns. They work to support other growing companies, ensuring the best for the buck!*
- Starwoks Coffee House
- DOMs Arcade *This is the place where video game players, from all over the country, come to challenge each other for top prizes!*
- Emptied Meat Factory. *There's nothing here. It's abandoned*

Methphodollous Island *Located somewhere close off the East Coast of the United States*
- Primous Facility *A facility that houses psychotic individuals who have had mental breakdowns, hardened criminals, and the like; there is also talk of the facility being used to hold cross-humans*
- Security Station *VLORs personnel authorizes access to the gates of Primous.*

Naphilia Town, Illinois *Forty minutes east of Hidendale Springs, IL.*
  - o A quiet suburbs. There is not much here. This is a just residential neighborhood.

- SpeedWay Rail Lines *SpeedWay Rail Train going in and out of the town.*
- Sysis June Lake *The beach where DiLuAH's ship crashed at night.*
- Clifaran Mountains *Ciemere Peak is the highest point and located on the center mountain.*
- E.X. PLODES Amusement Park *This ginormous theme park is currently being built. Projected time to be completed is sometime in the year 2108.*
- Fall Lake Retirement Home *Senior citizens over the age 70 are welcome.*
- Lake Meadows Apartments *Six floors of 3 bedroom spaces with one bathroom, one kitchen space, and a living area. Garages are in a separate building right next door to the property.*
- Ion Foods *Sells nutritional snacks and your regular grocery.*

Marina Bayou Harbor, Illinois

- o *Head south down Tarainound street. Three hours away from Hidendale Springs, Illinois.*
- Nelskex Park
- Starwoks Coffee House
- Construction Site: 'NEW! Suites Ft. Starwoks Coffee House' *Counchone Street.*
- A shipyard *Filled with tons of small fishing boats.*

Ococo Town, Illinois

- o *Drive on Wayworth Bridge to enter this town. The town is west of Tarainound Street, leaving Hidendale Springs, Illinois.*
- VeVideer Forest *A huge forest twenty miles from Hidendale Springs, Illinois.*
- Dokomo Park
- Starwoks Coffee House
- Casavol Beach *These are open waters (ships are free to pass through but not stop unless they're a small boat. The two piers are small. Civilians are welcome to enjoy their free time here with their families and loved ones. There's a few beach-styled restaurants near the waters.*

- Abandoned Warehouse *fifteen minutes away from VeVideer Forest*
- Old Carsodova Mansion. *This home is in pretty good condition. There's vines covering the entire house and stretching through the front yard garden that has grown expeditiously wild in under ten years being unoccupied.*
- Courtyard Gardens. *One Street west from the Carsodova Residence, lies the deceased family's former yard where they hosted many special occasions, including Bar Mitzvah ceremonies.*
- Courtyard Guard House. *Center of the Courtyard Gardens and behind lies old sewer systems leading to Gyrasion Providence, Gradelia City, and stretching farther out to even more exclusive cities and states far away. This was used long ago by founding families, but nowadays there's plants surrounding the area and no one living today knows about it.*

Gyrasion Providence, Illinois *Two hours and thirty minutes west of Tarainound Street*
- A seaport allowing U.S. Navy ships to dock because a base is located in the area.
- Medayo Drive *There are ten really huge houses. The wealthy lives here. Five bedrooms, three bathrooms, two kitchens spaces, a living area, and a dining area. There are garages attached to each house.*

Winndow City, Illinois
- o *A small city located right outside of Gyrasion Providence, Illinois. Two hours and forty minutes south of Tarainound Street.*
- Winnix Airlines *A small airport. There are a few airplanes that come to this airport.*
- Kaydale Hospital
- Starwoks Coffee House
- Vonrou Street
  - o Chochi's Convenience Store
    - ▪ Blanche Avenue
  - o Mars Millennium Apartments

- Ion Foods *Sells nutritional snacks and your regular grocery. Located on the worse part of town. On the verge of being shut down due to low numbers.*

Gradelia City, Illinois

- o *This city was built in the year 2019. This city became a major tourist attraction after the year 2030. There are many different restaurants, from every culture in the world.*
- NH Pharmacy
- Balibai Street
  - o Sushi Round'Omore
  - o Arrow Left → Tavern
  - o Ion Foods *Sells nutritional snacks and your regular grocery.*

Melaro Village, Indiana

- Juvenile Detention Center
- Starwoks Coffee House
- NH Pharmacy
- Ion Foods *Sells nutritional snacks and your regular grocery.*

Cauitry Town, Michigan *A very quiet town to live. The crime rate is down to zero percent.*

- Meliftorra Docks
- Crescent Boulevard *There are twenty townhomes, lined on both sides of the street.*
- Velneo Street
- Delrio Matte Grocery
  - o *At the end of Crescent Blvd, you'll get to Velneo Street. You'll have to turn left or right because it cuts through.*
- Starwoks Coffee House
- Delmont's Bank

Lamont Town, Michigan *One hour and forty minutes north of Hidendale Springs, IL.*

- Teekee Forest *A huge forest. There is nothing but trees.*
- Starwoks Coffee House
- NH Pharmacy
- Ion Foods *Sells nutritional snacks and your regular grocery.*

Falarbor Bay, Montana *A quiet place to live. There's a lot of boats and many fisherman.*
- Bayside Park *A children's park. Many themed fish slides and swing sets.*

Floraston, Montana *A lovely little town. A very nice place to live.*
- Moravale National Park *There's a tall building in front of it.*

Lake County, Montana *A moderately-sized city. A business area.*
- Lake County
- Polson Airport
- Ion Foods *Sells nutritional snacks and your regular grocery.*

Valey Sray, Colorado
- o *A huge valley of empty unused lands. There are no cattle or animals here. The land is occupied with nothing but palm trees that are spaced twenty feet away from each other. About twenty yards out, there is nothing but grass and the mountains lie past there.*
- Boosechaimou
- MieLiMeiLi Desert *This place resembles a large desert but it's just a huge crater-sized hole in the ground. There is nothing near this place, no stores, etc.*

College Station, Texas *A city in East Central Texas in the heart of the Brazos Valley.*
- SpeedWay Rail Stations *A station where multiple trains leave and enter from different cities and states around the world and the station, with tracks, connecting to Melova-Metro Train Station in Melovaton City, South Carolina*
- Stratum Oil Industries *Main Office Location*
- Stratum Oil Employees Parking Garage *Outside near Stratum Oil Industry's Main Office Building*
- Starwoks Coffee House
- NH Pharmacy

Port Aransas, Texas *A city in Nueces County, TX*
- Stratum Oil Industries *Fourth built location*

- Stratum Oil Conference Hall *Location across the street from the main office building on Duole Street.*
- Tektons Shipyard
  - o Dozens of boats are stored.
- Marc's Warehouse *This place has been deserted for years. This place is undergoing a foreclosure (starting in the year 2042) that has yet to be settled.*

Arnesto Capital, Texas *Island on southern Texas border, points to Baton Rouge, LA*
- NH Pharmacy

Varilin Capitol, New York *A new, small island city sixty minutes from New York City*
- NH Pharmacy
- Tipalerdale Manor
  - o *A wealthy mistress lived and owned this home (been in her family for generations) before she died, leaving the house to an Asian immigrant turned successful businessman, in a few short years. The businessman is a Mr. Cinah Nyani Eroiisaki. The man built many accessories to the home but there's some additions that are a mystery to the public.*
- Starwoks Coffee House
- Jake's Donuts Shop

Chribale Isle *A newly but small, secluded island near Sandulay Island. There's only a forest here.*
- An unnamed and uninhabited forest turned into SciQui's personal prison.

Merritt Island, Florida *Twenty minutes from Vinrail County, FL. via the Merry-Jorry Ferry.*
- NalVa Space Station: Ground Unit
- Mariberea Harbor Ferry Port *Take a ride on the Merry-Jorry Ferry*

Vantlonon City, Florida
- Toxic Waste Dump
- Transportation Express Bus Center

- Starwoks Coffee House
- Ion Foods *Sells nutritional snacks and your regular grocery.*
- Ever Wanderah Flower Fields
  - o *This is the main attraction to the city. A city filled with many different kinds of beautiful and exotic looking flowers.*

Lorelaville, Florida *Forty minutes away from Lake City, Florida*
- NH Pharmacy
- Nieu Springs Central *A middle class neighborhood with many houses and apartments. This place in on Babalou Avenue.*
- Starwoks Coffee House
- Babalou Avenue connects to Calamaz Street.

Vinrail County, Florida *A small railroad town. Few civilians living here.*
- SpeedWay Rail Lines *SpeedWay Rail Train going in and out of the town.*
- NH Pharmacy

Fuuluchi Capitol, South Dakota
  - o *An island city similar to New York but much smaller and more suburban. The city is media-based, everyone has some kind of talent... whether musical, art, etc. Everyone who is born and raised here has high hopes to making it big and traveling to Hollywood Vale one day to seek out their dreams. Hollywood Vale is located on Sandulay Island.*
- Melanie's Dance Theatre for Performance Arts
- NH Pharmacy
- Starwoks Coffee House
- Ion Foods *Sells nutritional snacks and your regular grocery.*
- Dwelco's Pharmaceuticals
  - o *The pharmaceutical industry develops, produces, and markets drugs or pharmaceuticals for use as medications. Pharmaceutical companies may deal in generic or brand medications and medical devices. They are subject to a variety of laws and regulations that govern the patenting, testing, safety, efficacy and marketing of drugs.*
- Fuller Street
  - o Saint Frances de Lou Public High School

- *The school is on Fuller Street, but he has to cross railroad tracks to get to the school. The tracks lead toward a bridge going directly over water to the next town. Rithmul Street is where he actually lives. The streets cross each other. Fuller Street is longer. The school is a straight shot from Rhin's house, approximately about twenty minutes away and the tracks is where the separation lie.*

- Rithmul Street
  - *A secondary Street Rhin's house lies on besides saying Fuller Street.*
- Nthorow Avenue
  - Leads to Aorthordocee Bridge
    - *Takes you off the island and to the mainland of South Dakota.*
- McGregor's Street
  - *Intersects Fuller Street, leading to the local school, Saint Frances de Lou High School, and the shopping center. Mr. Bhim Phantolok's place of residence is located here.*
- MiiChi's Vir-Cade
  - *A virtual arcade with more virtual reality games, including 3D augmented reality games.*
- RaisDale Plaza
  - RaisDale Cinema
  - Norisa's Hair and Makeup Salon
  - Chuck's Barbershop
  - T&N's Shoe Tailor
  - Starwoks Coffee House
  - VicLow *A designer shoe store.*
  - Chip N' Curry *Japanese cuisine.*
  - New-World Center Stage *Center Plaza, shows off new talents.*
  - Mitch & Mike's Emporium
  - Jack Burgers N' Aimee's Hotdogs
  - J&J Grocery
  - Skate O' Skate Rink Rail *A huge roller skating rink with rails used by extreme daredevils and large ramps for experienced skateboarders and bikers.*

HighTech City, Georgia
- Home to the HTQ Police Force
  - o **HighTech City HQ Police Force** --- lies in the center of HighTech City. The police force have orders, from Captain Sky Duebron, to protect the city and nearby towns. The whole operation is run by the Captain. The people under him are his officers, his operators, his detectives and his Junior Squad Division also referred to as the In-Training Division.
- GeoComm Enterprises *Second Built Location*
- Dutanburg Trail Park
- Techy Mountains
- Downtown Bus and Ship Port Station
- HighTech Central Plaza has a Memorial Fountain and a Statue of the Founder
  - o *The founder, Damone Allikust, is a war hero who gave his life to many Americans. He was a General in the U.S. Army. He moved on to serve as the first Commander at HighTech City's Police Force. He was the one who got a bill passed to start a youth training department, the JSD (Junior Squad Division), in order to train new soldiers and police officers. His focus was to help inner city children gain skills that will help make them excellent leaders. As a young man, he fought in a mystery war against the Jolt'Tweillers and the Shoc'Weillers. The President of the United States, at the time, kept this a secret from the public... that and a VLORICE agent got involved. BORN: October 20th 1987 - DIED: June 6th 2064*
- Information & Travel Building
- Editorial Office is located inside. *This is a small news and media firm. It doesn't do too well now that the Inquiziehion is growing ever so popular around the world.*
- Hii'Est Beach *Beautiful but has a few minor annoyances*
- Hii'Est Beach Café
- Hii-Est Pier *Near Tech-Trail Forest*
- Starwoks Coffee Mini-House
- Ion Foods *Sells nutritional snacks and your regular grocery.*
- Tech-Trail Forest
- HighTech Bridge *connecting to Curross Town*

- Transportation Express Bus Center
- HighTech University

Niechest Town, Georgia *The town is known as a flourishing Garden City. The town's growing every day.*
- o   *Border of HighTech City, north of Techy Mountains*
- Madam Urathane Alma's cottage is in Techy Mountain area.
- Neirolo Cavern. *An inter-dimensional gateway to the multi-worlds. This place has Transporter Relics inside the cave, buried under rubble. It wasn't intentional.*
- NH Medical Clinic
- Cheesar Forest with a Melody Lake
- M'Burgers 'n Shakes
- Starwoks Coffee House
- M'Burgers 'n Shakes *Opened March 2107*
- Mec's Family Bar & Tavern
  - o   *There's a small garden outside.*
- *le Restaurant*
- *le Cafe et tu*

Curross Town, Georgia
- o   Border of HighTech City, south of Techy Mountains
- Medical Facility for Psychiatric Help

NieCross City, North Carolina
- NiLum Facility Jail
- NH Pharmacy

Atlanta, Georgia
- Fish Market

Melovaton City, South Carolina.
- o   *There are three entrances into this city. When Melova Desert ends, you'll enter the city's southern gate. When heading out of Meadowy Way, you'll be leaving out the northern gate. The last remaining entrance is in front of NickelsFront Mall. This is the east gate. The east gate is between the other two entrances, left side once entering Melovaton City. Melova Square is the center of the city*

where the flamboyant mayor hosts events in the city. Melova Square is in front of the east gate and behind Melova Square is NickelsFront Mall.

- Melova Desert *The only way into the city. The South Gate is located here.*
- GeoComm Enterprises *The Main Office. There are only two in the United States.*
- Sysmosis Shopping Center *Groceries, Clothing, Everyday items & more*
- MelFlora's Talent Stage *A small, circle stage in the center of the city. Tourist Attraction.*
- Starwoks Coffee House
- Medical Facility: Psychiatric Help
- Melova-Metro Train Station *Ride anywhere in the United States.*
- Vale Industries-Corp: TRI Communications Department *Two locations in the U.S.*
- Meadowy Way *Way out of the city, located by West gate. Continue walking to Cattesulby Woods.*
- Cattesulby Woods. *Keep walking you get closer to Eximpplest Town, SC.*
- NickelsFront Mall *The East Gate.*
- Melova Square.

Eximpplest Town, South Carolina.
- Catsugue Forest *This forest is connected to Cattesulby Woods.*

Great Similiete, Nevada.
- Fort Oxnile
  o Naval Spec Ops Command Training Facility *Jayn's last duty station.*

In the year 2020, California broke into three new peninsulas, which drifted from California's original position. **Oirailie Island** is a new island that drifted north and is now the Northern California Peninsula. Oirailie Island's eastern beach points toward Washington State. **Sandulay Island** is the second newest island, which drifted west and is far off on its own. **Qudruewley Island** is the third newest island. It drifted southeast. The three new California peninsulas, all large islands, each have a Northern Beach, an Eastern Beach, a Southern Beach, and a Western Beach.

Oirailie Island

- Northern Beach *This beach is unkempt and dirty in the year 2107. It's been this way for a while. A hidden laboratory was discovered, after exploding, in the year 2082.*
- Eastern Beach
- Western Beach
- Southern Beach

Sandulay Island

o *The city of San Francisco is here with little to no change as in the year 2007.*
- San Drean
  o NH Pharmacy
  o Pellious Medical Clinic
  o Angelica's Rare Finds Shop
  o Starwoks Coffee House
  o T&N Convenience Mart
  o Hollywood Vale *Quite similar to the old and a more evolved Hollywood*
  o FropYoli Shop *This place is a local ice cream shop.*
- Northern Beach
- Eastern Beach
- Western Beach *This area is nothing but ruins of old destroyed buildings. Due to the destruction of the old Golden Gate Bridge, this island became lost to the California Peninsulas. There may or may not be humans who live here. There's a place where plants and vegetation grows, but this island is mostly uninhabited.*
  o Cremmosis Street
    ▪ *An abandoned convenience store boarded up with steel plates with metallic bolts.*
    ▪ *Sillieosis Pavilion Park*
  o Delloris Avenue
  o Ruins of the old Golden Gate Bridge
- Southern Beach

Qudruewley Island

- o *The two cities, Los Angeles and San Diego, are still very much the same as in the year 2007.*
- Northern Beach
- Eastern Beach
- Western Beach
- Southern Beach

To get to Marina Bayou Harbor, Illinois... Head south down Tarainound Street... Yeah! That long street. It is exactly three hours away from Hidendale Springs, Illinois. (If you are walking on foot.)

Miryova Price's Residence

She lives with her daughter, Jayla Price. The two live three blocks down the street from Zadarion's home. Miryova rents a space in the apartment building, near a suburban area.

The suburban area is a residential area existing commuting distance to the main street, Tarainound Street.

The building is painted a dark orange color, with white horizontal lines painted on building. The building is much larger than Zadarion's home. His home is a two-story house.

At Miryova's residence, there's an entrance in the front and through the left side of the building (facing from the street). There is one back entrance as well, leading to Miryova's handmade garden. She talked to the landlord about building a garden. Miryova grows distinguished and exotic flowers that are out of this world! They would make you believe you're living in Paris, France and various other locations. There is a minimum number of African Americans living on her block, Cenbaile Street.

New Waii Island is a small island located somewhere in the Atlantic Ocean. At the end of the twenty-first century (2095) an island lifted from under water in the middle of the Atlantic Ocean, right across somewhere near the south part of South America. A few people from all over the world flocked to and inhabited this new island. The island became overpopulated within a few short months. The island is believed to be the lost city of Atlantis that disappeared a long time ago. A few nonbelievers that say this is a fairy tale. The people of the new island are referred to as, Atlantis Dwellers. Within a year, a city was built. Still the only city on the island, it is called **New Waii City**.

Mount Caubvick is a mountain located near Labrador and Quebec. This is in the Selamiut Range of the Torngat Mountains. In 2015, Mount Caubvick was one of the highest points in mainland Canada east of Alberta).

Detroit-Windsor Tunnel was the fourth international border crossing between Michigan and Canada. This was not built as a bridge, but as an underground tunnel. It connects the Interstate of 75 in Detroit with Highway 401 in Windsor, the tunnel opened in 1930. In 2107, no vehicle has permission to cross this old international underwater crossing. The tunnel collapsed in the year 2040, creating a gorge.

Moose Mountain is a peak in the Sawtooth Mountains of northeastern Minnesota in the United States. The elevation dropped few feet (1689 feet (515 meters) in the year 2017 and currently 1574 feet) above sea level. This area is located close to Lake Superior and reaching 1087 feet above its waters.

Quad Cities. Around the compound of cities, at the Iowa-Illinois border, near the Mississippi River, this area includes three main towns... Rocky Pavilion (used to be known as, Rock Island), Central Moline (used to be called, Moline and East Moline but now one), Davenport, and Little Bettendorf, Iowa. These are adjacent communities.

In the year, 2045, Little Bettendorf, and the closer communities, went through many tragic earthquakes occurring in Illinois starting May 16, 2045. The shock which knocked over many brick-made chimneys at Moline (now Central Moline) was felt over 550,000 square miles and strongly felt in Iowa, Wisconsin, and a little bit in certain parts of Michigan. Buildings swayed in Chicago, but microscopic near this city. There was fear that the walls near the city's dams would collapse, but nothing too tragic happened.

Two months later and a second intensity VII earthquake struck on July 22, 2045, knocking down brick-made chimneys in Davenport, Illinois, and in Central Moline, and Bettendorf, Iowa. Over forty windows were destroyed, bricks loosened, and plaster cracked in the Moline area. It was felt over only 32,425 square miles.

On August 03, 2045, a sharp but local shock occurred at Vicpol, a small and quiet town of about 250 people. The magnitude three shocks broke chimneys, cracked walls, knocked groceries from the shelves, and contaminated the water supply. Thunderous earth noises were heard. It was felt throughout the Quad Cities, and all towns less than ten miles away (these other cities suffered little changes). Six aftershocks were felt. It is thought-provoking to correlate this shock with the May 26, 1909, shock and the 1968 shock (all had maximum intensities of VII, but two had distinctively large feet areas more than 250 times greater than that of the Tamms earthquake).

These earthquakes changed these towns forever. Molina became a barren wasteland.

Fifty years later, the year 2095, a Spanish drug lord, Aleixo Ricardo Adoración, brought tyranny to the area.

Despite it being uninhabited, Adoración, brought all kinds of people to this area. They were underground slaves, so no one knew about them. These people were on LOST & FOUND lists posted in almost every grocery store; a few from the United States and many from Spanish countries.

Sometime after VLORICE split into two separate organizations, the former VLORs commander sent an agent to bring an end to Adoración's reign. After that, the people there were free to live in peace. Many businesses were started, and everyone lived as merchants, selling to make a living with the goods they either found or made by hand. The United States Government wanted to help these people financially, but someone deep in connections with the president and House of Representatives somehow made them forget about the people in Moline. This place, currently, resembles Mexico in the year 2015.

VICE Basement *An unknown room where Scientist Mario Vega does his secret experiments and invents new technology. Mario Vega never sees the light of day.*

VH Universe Appendix Page 2

The V-Link *(see photo at the end of Book one)* is a high-tech digital watch that combines with the user's central nervous system. It transforms the civilian into his or her agent gear, is used to summon artillery and weapons, can teleport the agent, and is activated by the agent's thoughts and physical movements. Its features include:

- **Headset**. *The V-Link headset is worn on the forehead and used to communicate with people who are also wearing one*
- **V-Cuffs**. *A small, round, slick piece of metal that opens into a spiral and binds around an enemy to immobilize the person.*
- **Invisi-Dome**. *A circular barrier used to cover an area of a city or town, which cannot be seen by normal civilians and also prevents them from seeing what is happening inside the barrier. These keep civilians safe and prevent foes from escaping. Any VLORs member with a V-Link can enter a dome. Once activated, a dome affects all technology in the area, and any normal civilian inside one will have his or her memory of the experience automatically erased. Invisi-Domes also have restoring properties to fix property damage.*
- **Tiny Grenade Pellets**. *Exploding bombs that don't do heavy damage.*
- **Flame Igniter**. *Resembles a pocket lighter, but thin and long. It produces quick flame.*
- **Deflector Shield**. *A near invisible shield. Once activated, it's in the shape of a circle. Able to see through it and nothing can get through.*
- **Gasoline Capsules**. *A capsule that contains gasoline inside it.*
- **Holo-Messages**. *3D telephone calls.*
- **Q3 Explosives**. *Small devices that send sonic screeches to clear away particles such as dirt, small rocks, and the like.*

- **Q6 Explosives**. *Medium-sized devices that sends sonic screeches to clear away heavier material.*
- **Q9 Explosives**. *Small, cubed devices that expand and send sonic screeches that can destroy everything within a one-mile radius.*
- **Scope Lens**. *A tool that gives the agent the ability to see through walls.*
- **Tiny Daggers**. *Tiny swords for throwing at your opponent, used only by Agent Rahz.*
- **Tracker**. *A small disk, about the size of an American dime that, when attached to anything, allows the user to follow an individual.*
- **BIO-Beings**. *A new technology, not revealed until VLORs & VICE VOLUME II, was manufactured using Anaheim's technology. They are digital human bodies made to engage in missions as part of a project that was terminated after Curdur (an evil inside Agent Z) was born.*
- **V-Inducer**. *A small object that, when thrown, closes around an object or a physical being. Once trapped, whatever is inside the V-Inducer is destroyed by a blaze of fire. Nothing can resist the intense flames a V-Inducer can produce.*
- **V-Veil**. *A small, dime-sized coin. Once attached to a person, it turns them invisible. If the person is unconscious, they will remain that way as long as the device is in place.*
- **V-Haler**. *The V-Haler is a protective body suit, equipped to protect agents from terrible flames.*
- **V-Shield**. *An invisible shield that covers an individual, shielding them from bodily harm.*
- **V-Copier**. *This is a built-in function. It can produce multiple copies of anything, tangible or intangible. Although, the copies are like intangible objects.*
- **V-Absorber**. *This is a see-through thin blanket. Once it materializes and a person throws it, the very thin blanket unfolds and surrounds any kind of small particles such as... sleet, hail, sand, dust, etc.*
- **V-Line.** *A very thin and strong rope.*
- **TripCoin.** *Can change its weight.*
- **V-Cushioner.** *A small object, inside of a capsule. Once a person lets go of it, it can increase in weight. This causes it to*

weigh roughly about five hundred tons. It can later turn into a large seat cushion to soften a fall.

- **V-PoLi.** *A function in the V-Link. A general purpose lie detector test, enabling VLORs to uncover hidden truths. This function embedded into the V-Link, once attached to a body, can read a person's mind. It uncovers what's fact and / or deceptive.*
- **V-Medical Supply Kit.** *Primary medical equipment used in the field. This kit is connected to VLORs HQ's medical center database. The VLORs medical center has many items.*
- **Silent Dyber.** *A small device capable of blocking out all forms of noises and communication, including speaking and breathing, for miles.*
- **V-MeMinifiers.** *These are small earpiece devices that materialize into an individual's ear to block out annoying noises at high frequencies. These small devices work very well.*

VH Universe Appendix Page 3

NEW TECHNOLOGY

Creator... Scientist Rayley Nickolson

- **Scanner Satellite**. *A main satellite in outer space. It is cloaked and not easily detected. This is now separate from VICE. VICE is in the works of attaining their own. The V-Link connects to this satellite as well as VLORs's personal satellite that is attached to their base of operations... wherever VLORs HQ is located.*
- **Vactra Boots**. *Footwear with built-in gliding and rocket devices that enables agents to go airborne or to skate two inches off the ground.*
- **Vactra Flight Board**. *A glider that materializes from Z's V-Link and Agent Z's mode of transport.*
- **Vactra Sword**. *Agent Z's first sword. He is still a novice swordsman while using.*
- **Vactra Cutters**. *Lower left and right arm blades that eject from devices on the agent's wrists and Agent Caj's main weapon.*
- **Vactra Daggers**. *Sharp twin blades and Agent Rahz's main weapon.*
- **Vactra Blasters**. *A blaster every agent is equipped with. Emits a laser blast.*
- **Vactra Armor**. *In progress of being perfected. Arm extender with blaster. A metallic band that can expand, making an arm blaster. In the near future will be able to become a suit of armor.*
- **Vactra Bubbles**. *Transparent bubble traps.*
- **Vactra Boppers**. *Boxing gloves that pack a devastating, dynamic punch.*
- **Vactra Cycle**. *Operator Agent Rev. Travels through rough seas.*
- **Taser-Blades**. *These resemble regular Taser's but they're like daggers.*

Weapons Origin from… Unknown and now
disbanded clan of Japanese warriors.

- **Shibarion Blade**. *Agent Z's re-designed sword. His main weapon of choice.*
- **Shibarion Blade-Blaster**. *Agent CQua's main weapon. Able to manually change into a blaster or into a blade.*
- **Shibarion Swigger**. *Agent JeiFii's weapon of choice. Able to change into a V-Tracer and a Whip-like lash (think of a lion tamer).*

VH Universe Appendix Page 4

MYSTERIOUS AND MISCELLANEOUS OBJECTS

- **Repliara Crystatite**. *A rare crystal that copies a person's identity. If the imposter's appearance cracks, white lights expel out of the person who has taken another's appearance, returning that person to his or her normal self. The inventor is a mystery even to this day.*
- **The Flamethrower Unit**. *Built by Curtis Anaheim, The Fire Starter. Slightly resembles a normal MK-47 but it is much larger.*
- **SupeXoil**. *Capsules containing a viscous liquid derived from petroleum that can be used as a fuel or lubricant. The petroleum has been modified with an unknown substance. The scientist who created this technology is a mystery. This special oil was converted from crude oil to diesel fuel and then to an unknown chemical. It is used to power machines and only Stratum Oil Industries has access to it.*
- **SupeXelectric**. Capsules containing an electric substance used to power machines and created by Stratum Oil Industries.
- **Dale's QPad**. *A money transfer device used by Dale Jr. It is just an electronic keypad.*
- **ELiPiP**. *This small device (no bigger than your average cell phone) is a new unlimited power source that many businesses desire to have in their possession. It's clean, renewable energy. This device can receive and generate massive amounts of electricity within the programmed area.*
- **Silencer Stag**. *A thin needle-like twig-shaped object. If makes contact with the skin, one will pass out.*
- **T-04 Zero Memory Gas Spray**. *A spray that will wipe memories.*
- **Vex Armor Emblem**. *An item found by Agent Z and his little band of creature-friends during his time on planet Vexion.*

- **Opla Whistle.** *A normal looking whistle that can emit a silent sound capable of memory erasing.*
- **Paranormal Detection Reader, PDR.** *A device made by Louis Gravnelle. He built this unique device in order to pick up supernatural activity anywhere.*
- **The Cryo-Cap.** *A regular capsule with a coordinate codes panel embedded into the device. This can put a human in cryosleep (a state of suspended animation) and teleports individual to any location typed into its system.*

VH Universe Appendix Page 5

1999

- Krarnaca crash lands on Earth.

2007

- This year marked the end of the Shoc'Weillers and the Jolt'Tweillers, a race of lightning warriors and a superior form of homosapiens. A secret government assault was ordered by the president of the United States on December 31, 2007. This mysterious race of people had to be extinguished because they were a danger to mankind, according to the United States Military. Guardian Gai was attacked. He was struck by the deadly attack, The Deat'Low. This powerful attack can immobilize a person and it infects them with a horrendous illness. He died on October 1, 2007. Tundarick was also killed that same day, protecting him because it was his main job.

2020

- California broke into three new peninsulas, which drifted from California's original position. The three new California peninsulas all have a Northern Beach, an Eastern Beach, a Southern Beach, and a Western Beach. All three peninsulas are huge and contain many cities.
- **Oirailie Island** is a new island that drifted north and became the Northern California Peninsula. Oirailie Island's eastern beach points toward the state of Washington.
- **Sandulay Island** is a new island that drifted west, and is far off on its own. This is the Western California Peninsula.
- **Qudruewley Island** drifted southeast and became the Southern California Peninsula.
- A new island near the island of Japan was named, **Iitchii Mils** by the Japanese locals in the area. The Supreme Family,

Wasaki, lives here and rules the island with their elite troops of ninja assassin warriors. Today, the Leader of the Wasaki family has stopped all actions on creating order in Japan and Korea. He sits and relaxes in his castle. In the future, he will have a few children who will be banished across the globe for their terrible natures. In the future, one of his children, the youngest, will be the only one left at the Wasaki home.

2021

- A younger Asarios (Asari) and a younger Maleena (Malee) were sent to Valdesmon for their crimes, by the Great Wizards of planet Xeiar.

2030

- This year saw a marked rise in unemployment in the United States.
- Dale Falakar Sr. had four Stratum Oil facilities built in various places in the United States.

2068

- Madin Doro Torres was born.
- Richard Maxill was born.

2072

- Cinah was born

2076

- Xavier Marshall was born

2077

- Xanpo was born

2079

- Tundarick was reborn.

2080

- A mysterious sheet of metal crashed on planet Earth.

2082

- Samuel Marshall brought his six year old son Xavier to a secret lab on Northern Beach on Oirailie Island. The secret lab was destroyed.

2085

- DiLuAH's ship recovered from its malfunction in outer space, and his ship crashed on planet Earth near Sysis June Lake in Naphilia Town, Illinois. The ship exploded, and the passenger escaped. Miles away in Hidendale Springs, Illinois, where he had long been buried in a cave deep underneath the city, the cursed knight's tomb cracked open.

2088

- Xavier Marshall returned home with father after a long trip on their overseas adventure. Eleven-year-old, LeiSean Juhnen, appeared in the Namorant Dimension, on planet Vrec.

2089

- Thirteen-year-old, Xavier Marshall, fell in love with beautiful girl. Drey (Sirus Langford) was born. Michel Johnson was born. Cinah left Japan.

2090

- Jack McKoy was born. Ronald Osaida was born. Krarnaca, now known as Doc Krarn, was hired into VICE.
- June of this year, unemployment dropped 10 % in the United States.

2091

- Jodana Uvarla was born.

2092

- Jacque Baller was born. Joel Rodriquez was born. Lin Yiu Gustov was born. Gai Tunh Chi was reborn.

2093

- A war took place in the Namorant Dimension (Damonarian v. Quinoragoras). A few individuals, including Mayana's parents, arrived on Earth.
- Xavier Marshall collapsed and slipped into a coma. Rhin Kashioko was born. Jennifer Wayner was born.

2094

- Ryan (Zada) 'Z' Jones was born. Mhariah (Zari) 'Rahz' Johnson was born. Jayla Price was born. Kiyla Gerald was born. Alecxander 'Shocker' Jackson was born. Morgan Wiles was born.

2095

- A new island floated up somewhere in the Atlantic Ocean and was officially named New Waii Island. Rivi was born and later found on the island by elder Krojo. Valery Maxill was born.

2096

- Eraine 'Floral' Delpro've was born.

2098

- In the Namorant Dimension, the remaining Quinoragoras took refuge on planet Devina. They took over the Devion's home world. A young knight (Jaylin) was born. The mysterious cursed knight crawled out from under Drenden Mountain, located in Hidendale Springs, Illinois. The cursed knight explored this new world.

2100

- Mayana 'Maya' Johnson was born.

2102

- Young Alec was eight years old when he saw his mother's lifeless body dangling from a light pole on Sandulay Island.

2103

- Joel Rodriguez became a cross-human. He started calling himself, ShaVenger.

2105

- Dani discovered information about her uncle, Raymond Dilles, also known as, The Gallant Gamer. During the takeover of the twins' new virtual world, she uncovered the hacker's identity and what he's done in the past. A recent event mentioned why he was imprisoned at NiLum Prison and later released on good behavior in the year 2105.

2106

- Ki'liana (Kiley) Jones was born.

2107

- *Friday, June 9, 2107*, A Centransdale High School graduate, Morales Ewelling, stalks Mr. Anaheim and begs him to hire him.
- *Monday, June 12, 2107*, Donny and Sally knocks over Agent Z in Bayside Park. The park is located in Falarbor Bay, Montana.
- *Monday, June 12, 2107*, a young man, Agent Eron, is in the city of San Drean, located on Sandulay Island. He's enjoying one of his favorite treats inside FropYoli's Ice Cream Shop.
- *Tuesday, June 13, 2107*, Mitch and Rich are sentenced to do six months of community service and will begin their house arrest from June 13th 2107 to March 13th 2108.
- *Tuesday, June 13, 2107*, Unknown drunk driver who killed Brady Forbes and Michel Johnson will serve twelve years at Gowdon's Prison. The penalty is six years, but there were two deaths.
- *Thursday, June 15, 2107*, Mr. Sturgess McMillan committed suicide. He refused to be taken into custody after Agent Caj brought an end to the terrorist organization known as ZEXTERN.
- *Sunday, June 18, 2107*, Mrs. Amelia Daggerton dies in her home on Rouche Street located in Kale County, Illinois.

- *Friday, August 04ᵗʰ, 2107,* A medium-sized odd-shaped stone fell out of a portal after DiLusion and Commander Xavier returned to Earth via the same portal.
- *Wednesday, September 13, 2107,* Agent Z battled a new guy after defeating and destroying a mysterious new robot in Valousse City. During the confrontation, he deduced that Eron was wearing a special suit close to the ones him and Rev wear as VLORs agents. He plans on finding out the identity of this newcomer.
- *Wednesday, September 13, 2107* – Agent Z went to SciQui's personal island home and asked him a series of questions pertaining to the mysterious armband and the Vex Armor Emblem. He seems to be satisfied with SciQui's responses.
- *Tuesday, January 01, 2108* – Reesa McCulkin is hired at the InquiZiehion.

THE NAMORANT DIMENSION
There are ten planets, surrounding one lone moon. One planet was moved.

Junio's Moon
- Guardian of Malithia Reign's Here
  - o The center of Namorant and Pluto's *(The moon located in the Isolated Dimension.)* connecting twin.

Sol Moon
- Main Moon in Namorant and it acts like the Sun does in the Isolated Dimension.

Devlerlue Moon
- This moon is closest to planet Devina and only helps it out – providing energy and nutrients to plant life, etc.
- The time on planet Devina is based on the setting of the red and blue internal skies. The colors on this moon shift patterns, letting the Devions know when it's day out or night out. The sky remains dark and never brightens.

Vrec Planet
- Home to the Vrecians
  - o A race of Homo Sapiens that live above the planets core.
- Home to the Damonarians, morphed Homo Sapiens that live on the surface of the planet.
    - ▪ Crayos Forest is an ancient forest. Inside the forest is a device capable to transport an individual to other worlds. Located on the planet's surface.

Vexion Planet
- Home to many different breeds of creatures
  - o *PLACES*

- Maranious Forest
- Kilanene Valley
- Keikien City
  - King Keikaie's Castle
  - Keikien Lands
- Volsus Caverns
- Mooinz Valley
- Kepler Forest
  - Forest of the Fallen
- Vantronus Valley
- The Dark Land, formerly an empty field of grass. This area is now corrupted by dark energy. Anything that touches this area is changed forever. There's no telling how they'll be changed… either genetically or mentally.

Coroth Planet

- Home to Homo Sapiens, very similar to Earth humans but their bodies are more sturdier.
  - i.e. Kokashi, Dreyke, DomiNix and Xhirsten's new home
- o *PLACES*
  - Council of Coro
  - Methordarion Temple
  - Rapture Forest
  - Coroth Pavilion is the home where everyone lives. The houses are built right beside each other.

Vaoth Planet

- Home to Homo Sapiens with a green-colored skin tone.
  - i.e. Chloe, Prince Warzen
- o *PLACES*
  - King's Temple *(current King is King Diyas Warzen II)*
  - Rullie Lands are three areas of nothing but tall trees. These are homes for creatures living on the planet.
  - Vaoth Pavilion is the home where everyone lives. The houses are built right beside each other.

Naoth Planet *(New Coroth)*
- Homeworld to Homo Sapiens, very similar to Earth humans but their bodies are more sturdier. This planet is new. People living on Coroth founded and inhabited this planet. A female (Nical Winterl) had a few people from planet Coroth transferred to a new inhabitable planet, planet Naoth. She became the Queen. The current queen is her granddaughter. This planet is primarily ruled by females. The males that are born on this planet are sent to planet Coroth. It's like an exchange.
  - ▪ i.e. Quarah and new home for Goriah
  - o *PLACES*
    - ▪ Queen's Palace *(current Queen is Veriala Winterl)*
    - ▪ Diesca Palias are two areas of nothing but tall trees. These are homes for creatures living on the planet.
    - ▪ Naoth Pavilion is the home where everyone lives. The houses are built right beside each other.

Xirxion Planet
- Home to Xirxes Race.
  - o This world is a waste land. A laser was fired from an unknown location via space portal and wiped out the entire species. They're all extinct. There is only one Xirxes child that lives.

Quidior Planet
- Home to Quinoragoras Creatures.
  - o This world is a now a wasteland. A beginning to a Great Devastating War (Quinoragoras v. Damonarians). An uninhabitable world.

Devina Planet
- Home to the Devions
  - o A very peaceful but a small race of creatures. There is a small population of them.
  - o *PLACES*
    - ▪ Camp Qui (Tecquine Lands)
      - • Verrosl Stream is the only place to find water.
      - • There are no hills or mountains in this area.

- Quidior Capitol
  - Built in the middle of both camps in the middle of nowhere. A Quinoragoras tower where the revived King Gorvin spends most of his time.
- Camp Nor (Deckaquine Lands)
  - There's a small amount of water, inside the only two mountains in this area. This area is a harsh environment. Many Devions try to avoid coming to this area. If a Devion hangs around here, they're most likely trouble.
  - Somewhere deep underground, very close by, lies Dextorey's laboratory.
  - Frezarden Top is a tall mountain. It's extremely very cold at the top.

Xeiar Planet

- Home to all-powerful Homo Sapiens
  - o They look like Earth humans but their bodies store endless amounts of magical energy (Xeiar Magic). i.e. Wizards, Witches, and Oracles. There are also many monstrous creatures. A few of them are similar to those from planet Vexion.
  - o This planet is now a great distance away from the other planets. A magical barrier prevents non-magical creatures from entering this world.
  - o *PLACES*
    - Gateway to Valdesmon World lies behind Grand Xesus.
    - Grand Xesus is a meeting place for the Great Xeiar Wizards.
    - Council Pavilax is a stage-like area where the guilty (for any crimes) are brought before the Great Xeiar Wizards. King Makliton granted authority for the three Great Wizards to deal with the wronged.
    - Xeitri Lands are four areas of nothing but tall trees. These trees surround Grand Xesus. There are creatures, living on the planet, who make their home beyond this area. Xeiar wizards live anywhere they

- like. The majority of them live in-between Xeitri Lands and Grand Xesus.
  - Xai Pav is the home where everyone lives. The houses are built right beside each other.
  - McKelnor's Cliff
  - Valley of Blist
  - Los Xeiar is an area where the old kingdom burned down. What remains is nothing but old and torn down castle ruins. This area is a great distance away from Xeitri Lands.
  - MaKahMer Volcano is a long way from Xeitri Lands. It's all the way on the other side of the planet. There are trees at the bottom of this volcano.
  - Xanpo's Place is a small island near MaKahMer Volcano. It's a safe house. Sally and Donny's residence.

Extiepenia Planet
- Home to homo-sapiens whose powers derive from supernatural and paranormal forces.
  o i.e. Goriah's place of birth
  o They resemble Earth humans but their eyes are monstrous. Their eyes are alien.
  o Deep underground lives powerful ghost creatures, Penialia's. Once awakened from slumber, they seek an Extiepian and makes them their host body. Penialia's are transparent creatures. Their bodies are ghostly.

THE ISOLATED DIMENSION
This dimension is believed to be the center of the universe.

Earth Planet
- Home to Homo Sapiens
  o i.e. Humans, many different species of animals, and lots of different plant life.

Vegues Planet
  o 2,000,000,000 Light years away from Earth
- Home to Morphenile Creatures with purple skin
  o i.e. DiLuAH and CoLesTro

Kao 95th Planet
- o 2,000,000,000 Light years away from Earth
- – Home to Reptilian, many legged creatures
- o i.e. Doc Krarn

Vartan Planet
- o 2,000,000,000 Light years away from Earth
- – Home to Block, stony mole-like creatures
- o i.e. the former King Varnican

VALDESMON WORLD

The dark prison world is the ultimate prison used in the Namorant Dimension by the Great Wizards of Xeiar and other powerful entities. There were many creatures (aliens) imprisoned in this dark prison.

DARKEIL DIMENSION
A dark hell. An afterlife where the former living call home.

Everyone living entity from the Namorant Dimension believes Darkeil is an afterlife for all former living entities. The former living spirits have no possibility of a return. There is a slight possibility that a living spirit may still be alive if sent Darkeil by mistake. Everyone from the Isolated Dimension (especially on planet Earth) call this, Hell.

VIRT WORLD

A special digital world created by Dani and Rani Darivele, using a gaming console from 1991 they found.

LOCATIONS
- – Mill's Red Road. A long road (almost like Tarainound Street), connecting to many places. This is the one and only road in this digital world.

XEIAR SPELLS

Ventis – *Summons a cloud of paralyzing / sleepiness / poison smoke*

Nieeth – *Summons a see-through shield*

Nieeth-Thro – *Flicks away any attack with the sweep of a hand*

Gorgantro – *Creates stone pillars around a target and traps the person*

Nozespro Cuulazostras – *A wizard's special attack in the form of a BlastBeam*

Nozespro Cuulazostras Zestras – *A BlastBeam with electricity around it*

Blitargo – *If enemy is close, they are immediately pushed away*

Lita – *Illuminates the entire area within a fifty foot radius*

Cofrea Camoses Tarar – *A mixture of colorful lights and a barrage of attacks*

Healoris – *Able to heal a person but not the user*

SwiftRun – *Able to run at incredible speeds*

Deparo – *Able to disappear for seconds. Longer, depending on the user's power*

Cloudoose – *Clouds appear to create cover for escaping*

Scolifix – *A forbidden spell used to absorb an opponent's life force*

Fluse 'sposure – *A light brightens the area and brings an opponent out of hiding*

Wharsh – *A blast of water shoots out of the user's hand*

Vlornoc – *A spell that gives strength to the user*

Fileepio – *A wisp of fire shoots out of the user's hand to burn something*

Con para fornar recta – *Easy levitating spell*

Gorgo – *An easy lifting spell*

Bargo – *Fires a blast at an enemy*

Succuption – *Vine-like ropes close around an enemy*

Metio Verte – *A melting spell*

Con'tride – *Binds the victim in invisible ropes and tightens slowly*

Felieesous – *A levitating spell with a slight boost of power. It can also shoot an energy attack.*

Meschespa Vintigara – *Give life to plants. As an alternative, it's used as an energy blast.*

Vinlux Disparia – *Capable of making everything appear to be normal (someone who wishes to remain hidden).*

Quespri – *A transport spell only used to on planet Vrec and only used on transporter relics.*

Vin Lux Cumei – *Devastating spell that attacks the insides of an individual if used successfully.*

Bargo Excamei – *Utilizing another spell word, this spell can obliterate anything in its way.*

Mumeius Vecento – *Used to levitate user.*

Quipistorah – *A high level wizarding transport spell.*

ZesCuul Prelor – *A higher level blast beam similar but deadlier to Nozespro Cuulazostras.*

Mebictos Tencrias Oarede – *Summoning an inanimate object into a weapon.*

Vuevortis – *Torrent of water crashing. Multiple water strikes.*

Levanor Zhu Restural – *Healing spell.*

Nel Zul – *Works with Levanor Zhu Restural to undo binding spells, unlocks a source power.*

Respleta Espiliost – *A temporary binding spell, may be long term depending on user's power.*

Lutrids Spponallo – *Remedy destructive spells, turning the effects to normal.*

Parulliysis Sustotalus – *Paralyzing.*

Zracnqium – *Summons chains to bind someone.*

Rieeisco Vuesperusio – *Clapping hands together for thunderous ground tremors.*

Ignitiatious – *Lifting boulders from beneath and launching them.*

Xtermieyyo Celessisius – *A wisp of air coming from the sky to form a tornado.*

Depressislestitus – *Destroys and cancels out.*

Vobiiat – *Creating fissures in the ground below.*

Reec Gargantum – *Creating parallel lines of smoke forming by wind to act like blades.*

Levitaite Eniyeeto Tyrani Immedeni – *Powerful Terrakinesis.*

KAKLISTA
Kaklista is the ancient form of magic known to certain wizards, hunters, and huntresses. Kaklista is off-brand magic. A form of Xeiar spells.

Resposha – *A magical beam of light energy.*

Resposheer – *A magical barrier that reflects any physical being.*

Ranchuse – *A spell used to create a secure area, staying hidden. Can use for training purposes.*

Resmend – *A powerful spell used to make anything freeze in time for a few seconds.*

Mr Casey Mr Maxill
Techy Andy

Dave
Hailie
Mario Vega

Krojo

Rayley
Graizoid

Anbigala
Auntie Mama
Mr Del'prove

ShaVenger

Lin

Jaylin

CURDUR

Shocker

Floral

Flurir

213

Victor
McKnight

Dale Jr

Colussen

Adler

Stan
Bough

John
Talgitx

Curtis
Anaheim

KYROS-X Team

Mageario

Cloudis

Domos

Ron

Snake

Navas

Gobon

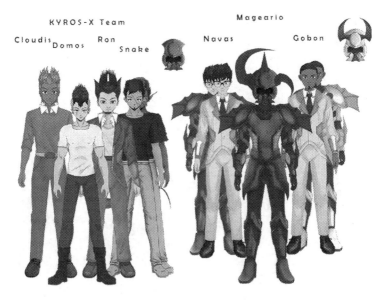

Kamalei Nakos

Morales
Ewelling

Maya
Cail
Adam

Mitch
Dave
Rich

Michel

Nathan
Katire

Rani
Dani

VLORs V-LINK

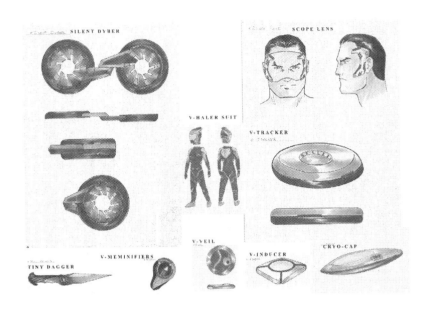

SILENT DYBER

SCOPE LENS

V-HALER SUIT

V-TRACKER

V-VEIL

V-MEMINIFIERS

TINY DAGGER

V-INDUCER

CRYO-CAP

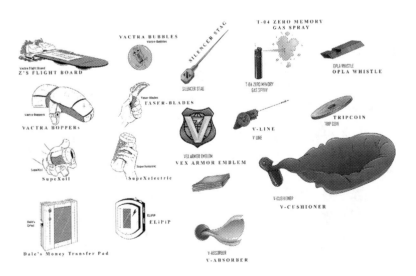

Z'S FLIGHT BOARD

VACTRA BUBBLES

SILENCER STAG

T-04 ZERO MEMORY GAS SPRAY

OPLA WHISTLE

VACTRA BOPPERs

TASER-BLADES

VEX ARMOR EMBLEM

V-LINE

TRIPCOIN

SupeXoil

SupeXelectric

V-CUSHIONER

Dale's Money Transfer Pad

ELiPiP

V-ABSORBER

216

Cordonald Miles

side head
view:

full
body
view

hmmm...

Principal
Hamul

Printed in the United States
by Baker & Taylor Publisher Services